BIBLICAL BETHSAIDA

BIBLICAL BETHSAIDA

AN ARCHAEOLOGICAL STUDY OF THE FIRST CENTURY

Carl E. Savage

LEXINGTON BOOKS

A division of
ROWMAN & LITTLEFIELD PUBLISHERS, INC.
Lanham • Boulder • New York • Toronto • Plymouth, UK

Published by Lexington Books
A division of Rowman & Littlefield Publishers, Inc.
A wholly owned subsidiary of
The Rowman & Littlefield Publishing Group, Inc.
4501 Forbes Boulevard, Suite 200, Lanham, Maryland 20706
www.lexingtonbooks.com

Estover Road, Plymouth PL6 7PY, United Kingdom

Cover image: "Bethsaida," Illustration 27B. Adapted by DreAnna Hadash from *Abbott's Illustrated New Testament* by John S. C. Abbott and Jacob Abbott. Originally published by O. A. Browning and Company in Toledo, OH, 1878.

British Library Cataloguing in Publication Information Available

Library of Congress Cataloging-in-Publication Data
Savage, Carl E.
  Biblical Bethsaida : an archaeological study of the first century / Carl E. Savage.
     p. cm.
  Includes bibliographical references and index.
  ISBN 978-0-7391-3781-9 (cloth : alk. paper)—ISBN 978-0-7391-3783-3 (electronic)
    1. Bethsaida (Extinct city) 2. Excavations (Archaeology)—Israel—Bethsaida (Extinct city) 3. Palestine—Antiquities. 4. Bible—Antiquities. I. Title.
DS110.B476S39 2011
933—dc22

                                                                2010048617

∞™ The paper used in this publication meets the minimum requirements of American National Standard for Information Sciences—Permanence of Paper for Printed Library Materials, ANSI/NISO Z39.48-1992.

Printed in the United States of America.

CONTENTS

CONTENTS

LIST OF FIGURES

LIST OF TABLES

ACKNOWLEDGMENTS

This work owes much to many others. Mention and thanks are due to a number of colleagues and researchers who have graciously shared the fruits of their labors with me. First I would like to thank those whose work I have incorporated into the present document. Sincere thanks go to Dr. Sandra Fortner, who was my mentor at the Bethsaida Excavations Project office, where she served for many years as the curator of finds for the project. She graciously shared her dissertation work on the Hellenistic and Roman finds that she catalogued through the 1997 season. Her compendium of the thousands of diagnostic shards was an important resource as I considered the more recent finds. Her work is particularly evident in figures 4.20 through 4.23 and tables 4.9 through 4.12, which depend heavily on her initial research, but her invaluable help in learning pottery recognition and discussions concerning the site cannot be contained in these pages. I would also like to especially thank Prof. Dr. Heinz-Wolfgang Kuhn of the University of Munich and his research assistants, Drs. Claudia Grüber, Regina Franke, and Steffi Keim for sharing the map of Bethsaida (see figures 3.1, 4.15, and E1.1) that he meticulously updates yearly and for other research material that he has shared. Additionally, I would like to thank the following persons for providing their research material that has been incorporated in the figures and tables of the book: Christine Dalenta, Hartford, CT, Bethsaida Chief Staff Photographer, figures 4.8, 4.9, 4.25, 4.26, 4.27, and several coin photos; Paul Bauman, Komex International, Calgary, Alberta, Canada, figures 3.2, E1.3, and balloon photography; Hanan Shafir, Ramat Hasharon, Israel, Bethsaida Staff Photographer 2006–2007, figures 4.24 and E1.4; Dr. Andrea Rottloff, University of Munich, Bethsaida Glass Studies Researcher, figures 4.12, 4.13, and table 4.5; Eric Stegmaier, John and Carol Merrill Qumran Project Staff Artist, figures 4.11 and 4.12; Dr. Donald Ariel, Head, Coin Department, Israel Antiquities Authority, table 4.4 and numerous conversations about the stamped handles and coins of Bethsaida; Dr. Arie Kindler, upon whose numismatic analysis figures 4.1 through 4.7 and tables 4.1 and 4.3 were constructed; Dr. Fred Strickert, Professor of Religion, Wartburg College, figure E1.5; Chris Morton (cosmo@cosmo.2y.net), University of Wisconsin at Eau Claire, member of the 2000 John and Carol Merrill Cave of Letters Expedition, co-developer and architect of the Bethsaida archaeological computer database system (Archbang), Appendix 1; Dr. Toni Fisher, for sharing her work and insights on the bone studies of Hellenistic/Roman Bethsaida; Chris Hetzler, for his initial work on the Bethsaida coin database.

I wish also to thank my colleagues in the Bethsaida Excavations Consortium for their work and encouragement in my project. I particularly am grateful to those with whom I have had the pleasure to dig with during the twelve years that I have been involved with the Bethsaida Excavations Project.

Foremost, I am extremely grateful to Dr. Rami Arav, chief archaeologist and director of the excavations. Rami has been gracious enough to teach, mentor, and discuss both archaeological method and the interpretation of material finds. His personal tutelage and his appointment of me to first serve as an area supervisor and later as assistant excavation director has been an invaluable experience for me. Our discussions concerning the many issues I have dealt with in my research have helped me to form many of the ideas that are advanced here. While we do not always totally agree on our interpretations of the data, we do agree on the value of Bethsaida for understanding the first century Galilee region and the value of continued dialogue concerning the implications of the archaeological record we uncover.

Thanks to members of the consortium with whom I have excavated directly and who helped hone my ideas in many ways: Dr Nicolae Roddy, associate professor of theology at Creighton University; Dr. Elizabeth McNamer, Rocky Mountain College; Dr. Mark Appold, professor of religion, Truman State; Dr. Walter (Chip) Bouzard, associate professor of religion, Wartburg College; Dr. Gordon Brubacher, professor of Old Testament and archaeology, Messiah College; Dr. Mary Patrick, Drake University; Maha Darawsha, University of Hartford; Steven T. Reynolds, Bethsaida coordinator, University of Nebraska at Omaha; and Wendi Chiarbos-Jensen, former Bethsaida coordinator. Also, thanks to many of the associated researchers with whom I have worked, in particular, Dr. Harry Jol, University of Wisconsin at Eau Claire, and Dr. Philip Reeder, University of South Florida, who have helped me to understand the dialogue needed between the scientific research community and archaeology.

The field work that provided the primary material under discussion in this work was enabled by the many volunteers who have taken their vacation time to dig at Bethsaida. Without the "Bethsaida Union of Movers and Sifters (the BUMS)" this book would not have been possible. My thanks to those who found unfamiliar objects and asked "Is this something?" during their time at Bethsaida.

This research has been supported by several grants and other financial assistance and I would like to thank the granting institutions and donors. First I would like to thank former Dean of the Caspersen School, Dr. James Pain and Dean Maxine Beach of the Theological School at Drew University for joining the Bethsaida Excavations Consortium, which enabled my continued access to the research materials at the Bethsaida Excavations Project. I would like to thank the Delmas Foundation for a grant that supported the work on the digitizing of the small finds and coins from Bethsaida in 2000 and again in 2001. It was during that time that I became familiar with the overall scope of the Hellenistic and Roman finds at the Bethsaida Excavations Project which led to the focus of this book. I was awarded the inaugural Priscilla Patten Benham Prize in Biblical Studies that was established in 2001 by Leary Anna Murphy in memory of Priscilla Patten Benham, a Drew PhD graduate. The Priscilla Patten Benham prize enabled additional travel to Israel in 2002 to begin work on the excavations in Area A West where I have concentrated my fieldwork for the last five years. I was also awarded in 2005 the Edward D. Zinbarg Prize, which was established in 1999 by Barbara Zinbarg to honor her husband upon the completion of his Doctor of Letters degree at Drew. It is a prize awarded annually to a student in any of Drew University's schools who has creatively linked Jewish studies and the study of other religious traditions. This prize allowed me to conduct further research to revise my work in the area of first century Jewish markers and the social relationships that were indicated by the material culture uncovered in the excavations at the Bethsaida Excavation Project.

As we all know, in archaeology the collecting of data is only the first part of the process. Producing a written record is of equal importance. I would like to thank the members of my dissertation committee for the invaluable help in shaping this book. The topic itself was the result of Dr. Herb Huffmon's lobbying me to change my dissertation focus after a tour of Bethsaida that I led for a group that was visiting various archaeological sites across Israel. Herb's guidance through the process has been enormously helpful. Dr. John T. Greene, professor of religion at Michigan State University, has been an excavation partner for many years at Bethsaida and other excavations. His sharing of his archaeological expertise and insights from his work at Gamla and other sites contributed greatly to my understanding of the archaeological enterprise. In the background of this work are the many conversations shared both onsite and in the off-hours of many summer dig sessions. I also thank Dr. Richard Freund, Maurice Greenberg Professor of Jewish History and director of the Maurice Greenberg Center for Judaic Studies at the University of Hartford, codirector of the Bethsaida Excavations Project. Richard, who possesses a vast knowledge of the formative period of Judaism and Christianity; an ability to foster the interdisciplinary study of scientific data, archaeological data, and literary research; and a willingness to share his research, has provided me with indispensable assistance in constructing this project. Beyond that, Richard has included me in many of the exciting archaeological projects that he has directed over the years, such as those at the Cave of Letters, Qumran, and Nazareth.

During the final stages of the writing process two persons played key roles and deserve particular thanks. One was Gloria Kovach, the office administrator for the Doctor of Ministry program at Drew University, who gave an enormous amount of time and energy in proofreading and formatting the written document. She also served as "chief nudge," encouraging me to finish the writing. The second was my sister-in-law, DreAnna Hadash, staff artist for the Bethsaida Excavations Project. DreAnna produced figures 4.11, 4.18, and 4.19 and revised the other drawings in creating the illustrations you find in this work. She also helped in tracking down sources and parallels for the tables. Without her assistance the finished product would not have appeared as soon nor with as finished plates as it now has. Also, I would like to thank Lydia York, PhD candidate at Drew University, for her hours spent reading this work and creating the index that appears in it.

Last of all I would like to thank my wife, Charleen Green, Bethsaida Excavations Project ceramic restorer, and our children, Natan and Itai, who have, hopefully, enjoyed living with me while on excavation, but certainly endured being left at home while I excavated. Charleen and I met at Bethsaida and so this project has been very much a part of our lives from the beginning.

1

INTRODUCTION

Mark Twain once wrote, "Get your facts straight first, then you can distort them as you please." As applied to archaeology, these words highlight the truth we all know. The data we employ in our reconstructions of the past are subject to interpretation. The way in which the facts are framed is vital to the way in which the data are understood.

In archaeology, we deal with the fragmentary remnants of human activity in the forms of artifact and architectural feature. As such we learn early on in fieldwork that three stones aligned together mean something. However, that something is at first only something to record; it is later that we begin to interpret what it could mean. During the later time is when one considers the choices, details, and life pathways of the people and culture we wish to know better.

Our archaeological model of culture recognizes the interdependence of four major cultural systems: technology, settlement and subsistence patterns, social structure and social organization, and the symbol system. These four cultural systems embedded in the matrix of time and space create the environment of the culture under study. This environment includes both the natural world and the presence of other cultures. We expect to gain insight from the material remains and their patterns to construct models of past cultures. This modeling includes the assumption that the sense of culture that existed in the mind of past individuals is reflected in the remnants that we find through the excavation process. The recovered material culture was produced by the behavior of the past peoples and represents the result of their action to implement their sense of culture. It is from this general model that we then go on to reconstruct how people thought, how they organized their society and environment, and how they communicated, internally and with other communities.

We seek to understand the thought processes of peoples of the past. This is not so easily inferred from the content and patterning of the material culture. However, from the designs, forms, styles, characteristics, and techniques of technology, we can begin to understand the priorities and values of the maker and user.[1] For example, from the range of possibilities, the cultural norm of a selected way of doing a task or designing a tool can give us an insight into the culture. This includes appropriation of technique or tool via artifacts from the range of contacts with external cultures through trade. Why this way and not that can be a telling elaboration of the culture.

Certainly, art and writing can be more expressive forms of culture that enable a reconstitution of the system of meaning that was the worldview of the past culture. But the complex nature of symbols and writing cannot be understood simply by decoding individual signs and specific documents. The deeper meaning of any symbol or piece of literature expresses something of the entire culture. However, the written artifact is likely to be more expressive of the understanding of elite members of a culture and not necessarily representative of a more general understanding of culture by the more numerous nonliterate members of the society.

Many archaeologists are convinced that the material expression of meanings and ideas can be deciphered, however difficult the task, and that the meanings and ideas can be somewhat reconstructed—cognitive archaeology. For example, by examining the surface treatments of artifacts or the embellishment of architectural features, one may explore the symbol system for design and learn the cultural values for art and design. Likewise we can draw tentative conclusions about other symbol systems such as: measurement systems, social relations, religion, planning and preparation for the future.

Yet, not all would agree that it is possible to gain significant insight via material culture into the beliefs, ideas, and minds of the culture that produced the material culture. Those who are skeptical of reproducing the thought patterns from the artifacts argue that artifacts are poor sources of cognitive data, so that any ideological reconstruction is nearly impossible on that basis alone.

Therefore, literary evidence has often been prioritized over archaeological evidence because it more readily supplies material that can be interpreted to create an understanding of the religious beliefs and practices of a community. Or, perhaps more specifically, because of the past paucity of archaeologically precise data, scholars are more accustomed to reconstructing societies by means of written sources. The role of archaeology, in this perspective, is largely illustrative and affirmative for these textually based reconstructions of the past. The textual evidence is prioritized, because it offers easier access to the worldview of the past culture, and material archaeology is assigned a supportive role.

This application of written sources to social reconstruction leads to many views of the "landscape"[2] of the first century CE, the textual topography.[3] For example, at one point along the spectrum we see painted a portrait of a Galilean environment "that was to a considerable degree dominated by the Greek and Roman mind."[4] Given such an environment, scholars have concluded that Jesus was at great pains to avoid the Gentile element in Galilee.[5] At another point along the spectrum others have suggested that only the "thinnest veneers" of Judaism was applied to the Gentile heartland of the "Galilee of the Gentiles."[6] "The claim is typical . . . a casual perusal reveals that many [scholars] report a strong gentile presence [in Galilee], sometimes a majority, sometimes a large and highly visible minority. According to this view, Galilee's large pagan population explains why Matthew 4:15, paraphrasing Isaiah, refers to the region as 'Galilee of the Gentiles.'"[7] What is lacking is any check and balance with the material culture that is found, a check that would measure whether the proposed cognitive system is indeed reflected in the material culture.

As a result, we often hear of competing mutually exclusive cultural topographies put forth simultaneously. "Pictures of a rural Galilee have stood side by side with those of an urban Galilee; pictures of a conservative Semitic society, with those of a Hellenized society; and pictures of a solidly Jewish population, with those of a largely gentile population."[8]

This situation brings to mind an analogy, a description of a hypothetical discussion between Tycho Brahe and Copernicus as they watch a sunset. Because of their disparate cosmologies they saw the same event but understood it differently. Tycho: "The sun is setting." Copernicus: "The earth is turning." Tycho: "No the sun is moving," etc.[9] From their limited perspective on the ground watching the heavens with the naked eye, they could but argue about their competing perspectives on the true nature of things.

However, as we know, neither theory was true. Likewise, the same can be said about the textual reconstructions of first-century CE Galilee. Yet as one begins to more fully understand the material culture, one theory will prove superior in matching the data and creating less problems for understanding the past culture.

"What does an overview of archaeological remains contribute to this discussion? Most important is the recognition that [the] material culture of 'household Judaism' indeed reflects behaviors and attitudes held in common."[10] That is, the patterns we discover in the material culture can allow us to see something of what was held in common, the consensual culture. This consensus may often pass below the threshold of display in the literature of the elite. We see beginning in the first half of the first century BCE and developing and solidifying into the first century CE markers that indicate a conspicuous self-identity for Jews in Galilee and also in Jerusalem. There is evidence from the material culture of a shared symbolic worldview, as Sean Freyne and others have observed.[11] In their daily lives most Jews were more alike than different among themselves, and certainly they were more different than alike compared to the greater Hellenistic culture around them.

At this point it may be helpful to give some indication about what is meant by Jews and Judaism in the context of this study. However, it may in fact be more appropriate to speak of what is meant by "Jewishness," since to speak of Judaism implies a somewhat more monolithic understanding of identity than was present in the first-century CE context. From the extant literary sources, there was not one form of Judaism if defined by theology. There was despite that seeming diversity, however, a relatively congruent core of life pathways. By "Jewishness" I mean that there was a population group that practiced a common life pathway that incorporated and yet distinguished itself from the larger Hellenistic culture. This constellation of observable practices is contained in the self-identity we term "Jewish." These behaviors can be seen in the archaeological record by the selection of artifacts by the group. While these traits might be characteristically Jewish without being specifically religious, there are factors that develop from within a common religious understanding that manifest in behaviors that may be witnessed in the recovered material culture. A commonality of material culture suggests cultural identity and continuity between Galilee and Judea. The concerns of circumcision, Sabbath and holiday, dietary observance, and connection to the Jerusalem temple seem to link "Jewishness" at the same time that they may be the points of diversity among the sub-groups.

There appear several distinctive self-identifying markers in the material culture: limestone vessels; the avoidance of decorated pottery; changes in oil lamp typology; the production of Jewish household wares that were mostly differentiated from their Hellenistic counterparts in the absence of decoration than in variation of form; absence of the cooking pan, indicative of a difference in ethnic cooking; and the presence of miqvot.

These artifacts and special architectural features illustrate a behavior pattern that can be seen as resistant to the Hellenistic patterning of life and indicative of a Galilee that is Jewish. They perhaps show as well a desire to connect religious behavior to everyday life, to use undecorated household goods that are therefore identifiable as Jewish goods, and in burial practices to preserve the household unit[12] (with the exception perhaps of Qumran and the Essenes at this point).[13]

There are limitations to this solidarity in Jewish material culture, however. The residences of the Jerusalem elite show a display of material wealth that imitates and appropriates far more from the Hellenistic culture, as in the use of decorated wares, the triclinium house styles, and grand mausoleum burials. These practices interestingly enough are noted and condemned in the gospel of Matthew 23:

> [1]Then Jesus said to the crowds and to his disciples: [2]"The teachers of the law and the Pharisees sit in Moses' seat. [3]So you must obey them and do everything they tell you. But do not do what they do, for they do not practice what they preach. [4]They tie up heavy loads and put them on men's shoulders, but they themselves are not willing to lift a finger to move them. [5]Everything they do is done for men to see: They make their phylacteries wide and the tassels on their garments long; [6]they love the place of honor at banquets."

> [25]"Woe to you, teachers of the law and Pharisees, you hypocrites! You clean the outside of the cup and dish, but inside they are full of greed and self-indulgence."

> [27]"Woe to you, teachers of the law and Pharisees, you hypocrites! You are like whitewashed tombs, which look beautiful on the outside but on the inside are full of dead men's bones."

Here we perhaps see a connection between text and archaeology, where text and trowel combine to show the contours of societal construction, the discourse of material display and disparity.

Without text, archaeological remains are often ambiguous enough to support a variety of possible interpretations. Without archaeology, texts are subject to unconstrained theoretical possibilities that remain untested. For scholars to deny a connection between text and archaeology creates an ambiguity in which evidence, data, facts, and findings can be interpreted in any number of ways. Granted, even making the connection between the two and seeing their complementary value it is still possible to interpret both the textual and archaeological evidence in different ways. Yet frequently one interpretation fits well with the majority of the dual kinds of evidence, thereby becoming quite convincing:

> Rather than testing theory against data, we can talk of "fitting" theory and data to each other. The process is one of working between part and whole, until as much of the data as possible has been fitted together.[14]

For archaeology, then, our best understanding of the past requires attention to this dual task. This would avoid the pitfalls of divorcing subsistence-settlement archaeology, field archaeology, from cognitive theory.[15]

This book seeks to aid the task by providing the archaeological data from tell-Bethsaida and suggesting its relevance for the reconstruction of the first century CE cultural context of nascent Judaism and Christianity.

BETHSAIDA AND GALILEAN CHRISTIANITY

> *For the most part, then, the archaeological finds from et-Tell do not tell us whether first-century Bethsaida's inhabitants were Jewish or gentile.*[16]

One of the ongoing debates in contemporary archaeological scholarship concerns the construction of the social setting of Galilee in the first century CE. Shaye Cohen frames the crux of this debate as the understanding of the basic problem of how "to preserve Jewish identity while simultaneously partaking of the riches of Hellenistic culture."[17] The debate forms in part as a result of a general shift in the field toward a focus on specific local and regional communities in their material, esthetic, and ethical aspects. This shift itself is part of a larger movement from history in general toward social history. For the study of the first century CE in the Galilee, this means that the context under investigation is not solely that of religious ideas but includes the geographical, social, and cultural world that shaped nascent Christianity and Judaism. However, the complexity of events that occur in that context and the modest amount of textual information from Palestine in that period, together with differing paradigmatic assumptions of the many participants in the debate, leads to widely varied reconstructions of that "Galilean home" for Christianity and Judaism. Several recurring issues appear: Who were the groups active in the region and what power did they hold?[18] What was the relationship between urban and rural areas? To what degree had the larger Greco-Roman culture permeated the average citizen's daily life?[19]

Most interpreters realize that the social, political, and cultural environments of first century CE Galilee provide crucial information for understanding the character of the New Testament writers/compilers and their communities.[20] Archaeological research is a significant tool for illuminating the everyday life of the ancient setting of the gospels, especially as the exploration of the Galilee region is continued. Combined with the literary sources that have long provided the basis for the foundation of the reconstruction of the social world, archaeology can help to explore how a group or a society acted, as evidenced from its material remains, and may also enable us to address what may have been the reason for such activity. The more we learn about Galilee, Gaulinitis, and Bethsaida, the less we need to rely on analogy drawn from other societies and other times to generate interpretive approaches to understanding the late Second Temple period of Christian and Jewish formation. It may now begin to be possible to frame our questions in terms derived from the indigenous socioeconomic organization of Galilee itself and from the projects of the people who lived and worked there in the first century CE.

Archaeology provides a significant means to recognize social, political, and cultural environments. However, from the outset, one needs to be cognizant of the challenges of employing archaeological evidence to understand cultural-historical contexts and so appreciate both the possibilities and limitations of this present study. All archaeological data is provisional. That is, on the one hand, more data is always possible. Each dig season adds to the accumulation of material finds. And, on the other hand, the data acquired is subject to multiple interpretations. Indeed, excavators themselves may change their own interpretation of dates of artifacts, the function of them, the use of architectural structures, etc., based upon newer excavations and/or further reflection and review in light of other archaeological evidence. One could think of the whole archaeological enterprise as one that is ever increasingly resolving the picture of the ancient past into greater clarity as more and more pixels are added to a digital image of the past.

These newly emerging "pixels" are made possible by the increased attention that archaeologists have given to the details of ordinary life that may be garnered from the artifacts. No longer are we focused on "kings and palaces, priests and temples." Analysis of faunal remains, grain, trade goods, religious items, coins, etc., allows interpretations concerning the interconnections between regions and cultures. In this study, we focus on the nature of society in the Galilee region as evidenced by what we have discovered at Bethsaida.

The Bethsaida excavations literature is now nearly twenty years old but in fact much of what has been uncovered at Bethsaida for the New Testament period remains unpublished. This in part is because of the recent focus of the excavation on the remarkable Iron Age finds, which include a palace, a well-preserved four-chamber gate, and a spectacular cultic installation in the gate plaza. In addition, the renewed scholarly focus on the social world of the Galilee has been in progress for roughly the same period of twenty years.

This rise in interest in Galilean archaeology is perhaps a byproduct of the abandonment of the quest for the historical Jesus. The preoccupation with the texts of the New Testament that dominated scholarship in the nineteenth century liberal quest and its focus on identifying the stratigraphy of the text had given way to a quest for the social history of the interpretive community. Robinson and Koester catch the flavor of this newer quest that traces the trajectories found in the text back to their common origins.[21] What remains, however, is a mostly literary enterprise that maps Jesus against a matrix of late antiquity filled with Gnostic and Pharisaic characters and caricatures garnered from other contemporaneous texts.[22]

This newer wave of interest, however, removes the canonical boundaries that may have constrained earlier attempts at locating the historical core. This is done not to observe the historical Jesus in the text, but to better reconstruct a community of faith and its formation by understanding the crucible that forged it. This is even still accomplished primarily textually. However, the textual information is now critically informed by reconstructions of the environment that produced the literature. Jonathan Reed suggests that this brings about the image of the scholar having pared the text via critical apparatus and form-critical methodology to isolate the core of "authentic sayings and plausible deeds" which are then used both to create a description of the reality of first century Palestine and to verify the designation of the deeds and sayings as authentic.[23] Thus, some widely variant "Galilees" are projected to have existed.

Reed creates a useful schema as to how the competing descriptions of Galilee may be understood. He proposes a "series of axes" that are useful in rendering the various depictions of first-century CE Galilee understandable in their various nuances:

> In terms of ethnicity, it has been described as Jewish, "Israelite," or even syncretistic and Gentile; in terms of cultural traditions and religion, Galilee has been portrayed as either conservatively Jewish or Hellenistic; in terms of economics, either impoverished or prosperous; in terms of its political climate, it has been portrayed as either zealously nationalistic or shrewdly acquiescent.[24]

Throughout the literature there are various perspectives on the nature of society in the Galilee and surrounding territories during the Hellenistic and early Roman periods. The importance of perspective on the identity of the Galileans determines how relations between Galilee and Jerusalem and Galilee and Rome are portrayed during the first century. These perspectives distribute along a spectrum that is anchored by the extreme positions of a Gentile, and hence pagan, majority to a ghettoized mainly urban/rural split between the Jewish majority and Gentile "overlord" minority. On the one hand, it is held that one should have expected a Gentile dominating presence, perhaps even majority, throughout the region with shrines and temples to pagan deities exhibited in a highly visible fashion. Scholars point to the Matthean citation of "Galilee of the Gentiles," found in Matthew 4:15 and presumably derived from the Hebrew scriptures in Isaiah 8:23 [9:1].[3] Thus, the Hebrew expression גליל הגוים is said to refer to the "circle" or "district" of the nations. This is taken to mean that gentiles from the surrounding nations had settled in the area. As a result, one could have expected a high rate of interaction between Jews and Gentiles.

There are of course numerous variants of this scenario. There seem to be two competing main views arguing for a Gentile population. One view, which traces its origins to the work of Emil Schürer,[25] and later Walter Bauer,[26] argues for an Iturean population that later converts to Judaism under Hasmonean compulsion. Recent work by Burton Mack may reflect this idea as well.[27] As one of the latest perspectives, he would reduce the racial distinction between the resident groups and attribute the social distinction to a religious preference alone. One, in this case, would speak of populations of Semitic-speaking people either Jewish or non-Jewish. Some using this perspective would therefore infer a "semi-pagan" Galilee.[28] So, from the thinnest of veneers of Jewish culture overlaid upon a truly Hellenistic society[29] the ministry of Jesus would arise.

The second main "Gentile perspective" is currently championed by Richard Horsley, although it too has earlier antecedents in the work of Albrecht Alt. Alt argued for the survival and continuation of Israelite culture following the Assyrian conquest.[30] This remnant cultivated its own traditions continuing the Northern prophetic tradition and covenental principles.[31] Horsley similarly asserts that "most inhabitants of Galilee were descendants of the northern Israelite peasantry."[32] Others, approaching the second pole of the spectrum, would argue for the exclusivity of the "Jewish context" of the area.[33]

The diversity of opinion on the question of Galilean identity stems mainly from the quantity and quality of the literary evidence that is used to reconstruct that identity. There are few relevant texts and those that exist are not without problems.[34]

My primary goal with this study is to supply details from the Bethsaida archaeological context that may be combined with the studies of other sites to produce a more detailed and therefore more nuanced picture of first-century Galilee. By differentiating between early and later Hellenistic and early Roman finds, this work may demonstrate that the population at this one corner of the "evangelical triangle"[35] was mostly Jewish during the first century CE. Also, it will explain how the transition from earlier populations of non-Jewish Semites and others to a predominantly Jewish population may have occurred. This idea for "Jewishness" in the first century CE is derived from the authors who are more or less contemporary with the period, Josephus and the gospels, and is based on four major concerns: circumcision, Sabbath and festival observance, loyalty to the Jerusalem temple, and purity, including dietary laws. The question to be answered, of course, is how to resolve the way in which these practices appear in the archaeological evidence.

The process of gathering primary data from Bethsaida has occurred in two contexts. One, I have served as Area Supervisor and assistant to Dr. Rami Arav since 1999 and before that as a volunteer excavator; and, two, a recent project of mine was the creation of a new database of finds beginning with the 2001 season. Prior years are being added to this new database from an earlier format. The kinds of data gathered in both contexts include the actual finds, site drawings, and field notes. A digital photographic database of loci data has been completed for 1997–2006 and will eventually include all previous years. The prior diagnostics and finds must currently be accessed onsite at the Beit Yigal Allon Museum in Ginosar, Israel.

Because of the nature of archaeological argument from the slim residues of cultural behaviors found in limited numbers of recovered artifacts, one must be circumspect when interpreting toward a given hypothesis. The danger is in arguing selectively from the record and ignoring data that does not fit one's desired view of the first century CE context. Also, one may tend to attach a substantiation of behavior or belief to a single artifact. I will demonstrate this type of argumentation with an absurd example. We find at Bethsaida many flint blades. There could be a temptation to jump to the conclusion that the presence of flint blades is indicative of the practice of circumcision and Jewish presence, since flint blades are prescribed for that activity. Other sites with no flint blades would suggest a non-Jewish site. This, of course, is a leap far beyond many plausible alternative explanations.[36]

The example also indicates a common misuse of the archaeological record. When I stated that we found flint blades at Bethsaida, I did not mention what period of time they were associated with. That is, it is important always to remember that archaeology has a "z-axis" of location of material. One works in the horizontal plane of geographical relationship and a vertical plane of time displacement. Simply put, material on the bottom layer is older than that deposited above, the law of superposition. There are of course exceptions to the simple statement of the law because of inversions of material caused by various actions or physical processes. For example, inversions of position could be caused by the digging of pits in the accumulations by human or animal activity, or the process of erosion on a tel's slope. But the general principle remains. Yet, lumping all artifacts together regardless of their chronological location is a practice often found in reconstructions of the first century CE. The first century is clustered with the surrounding centuries. Thus the chronological cues of transition are lost and the overall archaeological context is muddled.

What is clear at Bethsaida, however, is that when one examines the entire archaeological context of the site a well-defined shift from one cultural orientation to another occurs during the transition from Hellenistic to early Roman periods. The nature of the data does not allow us to speculate as to a precise ratio of Jews to non-Jews, but one can discern a change in interaction from the "pagan" northern coastal cities to the Jewish south.

Noting the shift in majority orientation, however, does not immediately lead to the determination of Jewish/non-Jewish interaction. Nor does it necessarily lead to understanding the culture's response toward the Greco-Roman influence. Thus, issues such as the possibility of the roaming cynic philosopher cannot be determined from the archaeological record with any confidence since it is almost never possible to ascertain the presence of relatively small groups. *Yet, whatever happened within Bethsaida in the first century CE, gentiles seem to have left only a very modest impact on the archaeological record.*

This lack of gentile presence makes several approaches to understanding the social context of Galilee suspect. Those who base their idea of first century CE Galilee on general characteristics of the Hellenistic Age may find that the Galilee does not share as many of these characteristics as previously thought. But this is only a secondary consequence of this archaeological study of the first century CE context. The social scientific studies that examine urban/rural interactions, for example, may need to be re-examined in light of an apparent significant relationship between rural and urban population centers that is seen at Bethsaida.

Finally, building arguments literally from the ground up, that is, starting with archaeological excavations and building a larger picture from their combined findings, may prove to be the more fruitful approach in the future. Archaeology in dialogue with the more classic disciplines employed by scholars of the New Testament and early Judaism may show that Hellenism had influenced some forms of expression but not necessarily the entirety of the cultural content of the region.

This study seeks to enter that process of constructing a portrait of Galilee, drawing from archaeological evidence at et-Tell, commonly identified as Bethsaida,[37] a place named in the gospels and Josephus. It attempts to view the role of the ancient inhabitants of Galilee in creating material practices that are indications of their sense of "place" both ideologically and geographically. They were involved in creating, accommodating, and resisting the competing influences and powers that shaped their first century CE world. Essentially, it is that world that the various attempts at reconstruction of the first century CE seek to approximate.

In the second chapter, I will review images of the first-century CE Galilean context, first delineating the territory in question, then identifying the bases of others' contentions for either a large number of gentiles or Jews, arguments that derive in part from the larger historical record of conquest in the region. The Galilee and surrounding territory was repeatedly subjected to rule by foreign powers. Thus a "mixed" racial, and thereby mixed religious, composition is presumed by many to be obvious. Secondly, the prevalent understanding of trade based upon analogical constructions from other, often later, periods assumes that the presence of Roman trade routes is indicative of an increased presence of foreign traders and travelers. Consequently, the general literature reflects the perception that archaeological finds attest to a diversity of peoples in first century CE Galilee.

The third chapter offers an overview of the political and demographic history of the region. This is key to understanding the changes in population that must have occurred from the Assyrian conquest to the end of the early Roman period, changes that, of course, would impact the first century CE context of Bethsaida. In particular, the effects of the constant warfare throughout the region experienced during the Hellenistic period will be explored.

The fourth chapter presents the material record of finds for first century CE Bethsaida. It provides a comprehensive look at the artifacts and architectural structures.

The fifth chapter develops the implications of the findings from Bethsaida for the evaluation of the historical plausibility of various social reconstructions of the region in the first century CE. The conclusion summarizes the extent of and response to Greco-Roman influence in the Galilean region as evidenced at Bethsaida.

When the data has been thoroughly reviewed, the image of first century CE Bethsaida that emerges is one that is at home in the gallery of a Jewish Galilee. Far from being subdued and dominated by a harsh anti-Jewish Hellenism, one finds a community that is mostly Jewish and that expresses its life pathways via contemporary cultural forms.

NOTES

1. Miriam T. Stark, "Technical Choices and Social Boundaries in Material Culture Patterning: An Introduction," in *The Archaeology of Social Boundaries*, ed. Miriam T. Stark, Smithsonian Series in Archaeological Inquiry (Washington, DC: Smithsonian Institution Press, 1998), 1–11.

2. James Strange following Marianne Sawicki notes concerning Josephus' view of the Galilee: "Josephus' description of Galilee in the *Vita* exhibits a kind of urban bias, if you will, a detectable 'mindscape.'" He holds that Josephus is not interested in portraying the geophysical landscape or simply the social-economic relationships among the parties inhabiting Galilee. Rather he intends to portray two main cities of Galilee, Sepphoris and Tiberias, as the place where "he acted out his roles as general, aristocrat, and representative of virtue." James F. Strange, *Sepphoris and Galilee in Josephus' Vita*, Papers of the SBL Josephus Seminar, 1999–2004 (2001), http://pace.cns.yorku.ca:8080/media/pdf/sbl/strange2001.pdf (accessed August 23, 2007).

3. Marianne Sawicki, *Crossing Galilee: Architectures of Contact in the Occupied Land of Jesus* (Harrisburg, PA: Trinity Press International, 2000), 37; Sean Freyne, "Galilee-Jerusalem Relations According to Josephus' Life," *New Testament Studies* 33 (1987): 600–609. Both authors examine the idea of any depiction of landscape as "mindscape," that is, a presentation of geography that also portrays the cultural understanding of it.

4. Abraham J. Malherbe, "Life in the Greco-Roman World," in *The World of the New Testament* (Austin, TX: R. B. Sweet Co., Inc., 1967), 4.

5. Malherbe, "Life in the Greco-Roman World," 5.

6. Burton L. Mack, *The Lost Gospel: The Book of Q & Christian Origins* (San Francisco: HarperSanFrancisco, 1993).

7. Mark A. Chancey, *The Myth of a Gentile Galilee: The Population of Galilee and New Testament Studies* (New York: Cambridge University Press, 2002), 15. Mark Chancey notes two works that summarize and support this view: G. H. Boobyer, *Galilee and Galileans in St. Mark's Gospel* (1953), 334–58; and Bo Ivar Reicke, *The New Testament Era: The World of the Bible from 500 B.C. to A.D. 100* (Philadelphia: Fortress Press, 1968), 117.

8. Chancey, *The Myth of a Gentile Galilee: The Population of Galilee and New Testament Studies*, 3.

9. This account of a hypothetical conversation was one that I read or heard during my undergraduate years, but I have since been unable to locate its source.

10. Andrea M. Berlin, *Jewish Life Before the Revolt: The Archaeological Evidence*, Papers of the SBL Josephus Seminar, 1999–2004 (2004), 48, http://pace.cns.yorku.ca:8080/media/pdf/sbl/Berlin%20Archaeology.pdf (accessed August 23, 2007).

11. See, for example, Freyne, "Galilee-Jerusalem Relations According to Josephus' Life."

12. Berlin, *Jewish Life Before the Revolt: The Archaeological Evidence*, 11.

13. The author's own research at Qumran included mapping the cemetery. The form of burial in the large cemetery seems peculiar to the Qumran area: single body burials without grave goods in a n/s orientation with heaped stones and head and foot stones as markers. See Philip Reeder, Harry Jol, Richard Freund, and Carl Savage, "Geoarchaeology of the Qumran Archaeological Site, Israel," *Focus on Geography* 48, no. 1 (Summer 2004): 12–19.

14. Robert W. Preucel and Ian Hodder, *Contemporary Archaeology in Theory: A Reader*, ed. Robert W. Preucel, Social Archaeology (Cambridge, MA: Blackwell, 1996), 10. See also Lewis Binford's chapter on "Translating the Archaeological Record" in Lewis Roberts Binford, John F. Cherry, and Robin Torrence, *In Pursuit of the Past: Decoding the Archaeological Record*, ed. John F. Cherry (New York and London: Thames and Hudson, 1983), 19–30.

15. "When we see cosmology derived solely from the alleged orientation of a building to a particular star, when we see ancient religion constructed from a handful of figurines or the red dado painting on the wall of a shrine, we have a right to be skeptical. Equally troubling is the notion . . . that the quality of a theory is to be measured by its style and flair, rather than to the extent to which it is grounded in evidence." Kent V. Flannery and Joyce Marcus, "Cognitive Archaeology," in *Contemporary Archaeology in Theory: A Reader*, ed. Robert W. Preucel, Social Archaeology (Cambridge, MA: Blackwell, 1996), 361.

16. Chancey, *The Myth of a Gentile Galilee: The Population of Galilee and New Testament Studies*, 108.

17. Shaye J. D. Cohen, *From the Maccabees to the Mishnah*, Library of Early Christianity (Philadelphia: Westminster Press, 1987), 37.

18. This discussion is also reflected in the arguments of textual interpreters. Anthony J. Saldarini noted that most studies on Matthew also concentrate on the population matrix of Matthew's community and its self-identification vis-á-vis the larger social context. He argues that Matthew's group was a small minority group within the first-century CE Jewish community of the eastern Mediterranean. But he asserts that the "usual understandings" of what first-century Judaism was like must be modified to actually fit the first century. Anthony J. Saldarini, *Matthew's Christian-Jewish Community*, Chicago Studies in the History of Judaism (Chicago: University of Chicago Press, 1994), 2–3, 12f.

19. Classic studies, such as that by Martin Hengel, *Judaism and Hellenism Studies in Their Encounter in Palestine during the Early Hellenistic*

Period (London: SCM Press, 1974), were often the underpinning for many reconstructions of the social community of the gospel writers. Howard Clarke Kee is a good example of this sort of development, where he relies on Hengel's discourse on the patterns of social dynamics during the "crisis that arose during the period of Ptolemaic domination." Referring to Hengel, Kee notes that despite "regrettably sparse evidence," he is able to depict the socioeconomic conditions and illuminate the social repercussions of Hellenization. Howard Clark Kee, *Community of the New Age Studies in Mark's Gospel* (Philadelphia: Westminster Press, 1977), 79f.

20. One can look to various New Testament introductions to see this pattern. For example, Pheme Perkins has a chapter on "The World of Jesus" in which she maps out "[s]ome of the political realities of that time." She does not cite her sources for this reconstruction but nonetheless it is important enough to be given as background for the setting of the book. Pheme Perkins, *Reading the New Testament: An Introduction* (New York: Paulist Press, 1988), 23–50.

21. "Understanding this process [of the history of early Christian communities] requires critical judgment as well as the construction of trajectories through the history of early Christianity." Helmut Koester, *Introduction to the New Testament* (New York: Walter de Gruyter, 1995), xiv. See also James McConkey Robinson and Helmut Koester, *Trajectories Through Early Christianity* (Philadelphia: Fortress Press, 1971).

22. John P. Meier ably outlines the common literary sources for this type of re-creation of a historical Jesus. John P. Meier, *A Marginal Jew: Rethinking the Historical Jesus*, The Anchor Bible Reference Library (New York: Doubleday, 1991).

23. Jonathan L. Reed, *Archaeology and the Galilean Jesus: A Re-Examination of the Evidence* (Harrisburg, PA: Trinity Press International, 2000), 1–3. His entire chapter one is a very good overview of the relationship between textual and archaeological study of the first century. See also John Dominic Crossan and Jonathan L. Reed, *Excavating Jesus Beneath the Stones, Behind the Texts* (San Francisco: HarperSanFrancisco, 2001), where they seek to integrate the two more fruitfully.

24. Reed, *Archaeology and the Galilean Jesus: A Re-Examination of the Evidence*, 8.

25. Emil Schürer, Géza Vermès, and Fergus Millar, *The History of the Jewish People in the Age of Jesus Christ (175 B.C.–A.D. 135)*, ed. Géza Vermès (Edinburgh: Clark, 1973).

26. Walter Bauer, "Jesus der Galiläer," in *Aufsätze und Kleine Schriften,* ed. Georg Strecker (Tübingen: Mohr Siebeck, 1967), 91–108.

27. Mack, *The Lost Gospel: The Book of Q & Christian Origins,* 51–68.

28. Robert Walter Funk, *Honest to Jesus: Jesus for a New Millennium* (San Francisco: HarperSanFrancisco, 1996), 79.

29. Mack, *The Lost Gospel: The Book of Q & Christian Origins,* 79.

30. See Albrecht Alt, "Galiläische Probleme," in *Kleine Schriften Zur Geschichte Des Volkes Israel* (München: C.H. Beck, 1953), 2:363–465.

31. Francis Loftus reiterates Alt's view in an article in *Jewish Quarterly Review*: "Recent work on the Assyrian conquests has shown that the Assyrians did not totally depopulate the areas they conquered and repopulate them with foreigners, and did not wipe out local cults. Several scholars have asserted that the great mass of the peasant population would have hardly felt the change of government. Thus it may be assumed that Israelite tradition continued throughout the Assyrian period." Francis Loftus, "The Anti-Roman Revolts of the Jews and the Galileans," *The Jewish Quarterly Review* 68, no. 2 (October 1977): 78–79.

32. Richard A. Horsley, *Galilee History, Politics, People* (Valley Forge, PA: Trinity Press International, 1995), 40.

33. As does Mark A. Chancey, who states, "We must always keep in mind the region's predominately Jewish milieu." Chancey, *The Myth of a Gentile Galilee: The Population of Galilee and New Testament Studies,* vii.

34. These sources include the Maccabean books, Josephus' writings, the Gospel literature, and rabbinic texts.

35. The "evangelical triangle" is the approximately twenty-kilometer triangle formed by the three ancient cities of Bethsaida, Chorazin, and Capernaum where most of Jesus' teachings were said to have taken place.

36. Two possibilities from among many are the use of flint blades for sacrifice, or their use in industry, perhaps in tanning. See Richard A. Freund, "The Tannery of Bethsaida?" in *The Bethsaida Excavations Project Reports & Contextual Studies, Vol. 3,* ed. Rami Arav (Kirksville, MO: Truman State University Press, 2004), 233–52.

37. See Excursus 2 for an overview of the arguments supporting this identification.

2

BETHSAIDA IN THE "GALILEES"

Galilee of the gentiles—That part of Galilee which lay beyond Jordan was so called, because it was in great measure inhabited by gentiles, that is, heathens.[1]

If you look at most maps of Galilee created to describe the borders between Jews and Gentiles, you will not usually find Bethsaida listed. On the one hand, this is not surprising since often Bethsaida is not considered to be technically part of the Galilee. Mainly this is because it is traditionally situated on the eastern side of the Jordan River. While there is at least one author who designated Galilee as the circuit around the Kinneret, that would seem to be a unique understanding of the term. Most scholars point to the term "Galilee" as describing the region to the west of the Kinneret and extending to the coastal regions to the west, to Syria in the north, and to Samaria in the south. It is also similarly described with a bit more precision as the northern region of Judea (Israel, Palestine) that is bounded to the east by the river Jordan and Lake Gennesaret (the Kinneret, the Sea of Galilee), to the north by the Leontes river (Litani), to the west by Phoenicia, and to the south by Samaria.[2] On the other hand, Gamla frequently appears on maps of the Galilee and yet it is even farther to the east than Bethsaida (et-Tell). That inclusion would seem to indicate some understanding of Galilee as a region that should include all Jewish settlements in the adjacent territory as well. This is somewhat more than a geographical understanding but includes an ethnic component, which, as we will see below, is often a part of any understanding of the Galilee.

Jack Finegan, in his discussion of Bethsaida, states that the Gospel of John's comment in 12:21[3] indicates that Bethsaida was loosely regarded as belonging to Galilee.[4] This view of "loose incorporation" finds support in the writings of the second century CE geographer Claudius Ptolemy who in his *Geographia* considers Julius (i.e., Bethsaida) as one of the "four main cities of Galilee."[5] Nevertheless, Josephus, contemporary to the first century Galilee we are examining, does not mention Bethsaida as a leading city, although he certainly considers it as within the Jewish territory. James Strange concludes that Josephus considers only the larger cities on the western side of the Kinneret as leading cities, particularly Sepphoris and Tiberias, although sometimes he included the cities of Gabara and Taricheae in an expanded list of four leading cities. Bethsaida, of course, is mentioned by Josephus as a Jewish territory, but not as a leading city of Galilee. This may be because it was indeed not as large as any of the four he does deem leading cities, or because he understood that although Jewish, Bethsaida was not "in Galilee."[6]

So the question of the understanding of the borders of the Galilee region may be important for our understanding of both Bethsaida's relationship to the region and to the understanding about the socioeconomic and cultural aspects of the region. It is important, however, to distinguish the region carefully by time period, rather than assume that the area remains consistently the same. For our purpose, Bethsaida needs to be placed in relation to the "classical period" of the Hellenistic/Roman times and not to either the earlier Iron Age or Persian periods or the later Byzantine period.

Sean Freyne outlines the boundaries for the area known as the Galilee as follows: "a central hill country surrounded by markedly different physical features—a coastal plain linked with harbors, a large inland plain, unusual for Palestine, and a rift comprised of river and lake, the only navigable waterway in inland Palestine."[7]

Zvi Gal, describing the Iron Age Lower Galilee, determines the boundaries with somewhat more precision:

> Lower Galilee is the lower segment of the northern hilly district in Israel. Its southern border stretches along the northern length of the Harod and Beth-Shean valleys in the east, to Gibat Hammoreth in the west. From here, the border continues to the foothills of the Nazere-than ridge, from Tabor in the east to Shimron in the west.... The eastern border of Lower Galilee is identified by the sharp escarpment of Ramat Issachar, Yabnael, and the Arbel heights. From the Arbel peak the border wends westward to the fringes of the Haqoq hills, including the Ginosar Valley as part of the Jordan Valley. It follows the Kinnereth shore, finally joining the prominent border of Nahal Ammud.[8]

Thus, Gal and others do not extend the Galilee to the western shore of the lake during the Iron Age. However, Salomon Grootkerk in his toponymic gazetteer does include Bethsaida in the Galilee during the "classical period," the Hellenistic/Roman period.[9] There is an apparent expansion of the Jewish territory beyond its older Iron Age range during the later Hellenistic period. L. E. Elliot-Binns likewise cites the Mishnah for a three-fold division of the Galilee during the classical period into Upper, Lower, and Valley districts. The Valley is defined as that "part around Tiberias."[10] Yet, it is somewhat unclear whether or not Elliott-Binns would include Bethsaida in the "Valley."[11]

Mordechai Aviam, discussing the borders between Jews and Gentiles in the Galilee during the classical periods, notes: "During the period between the conquest of the Galilee by the Assyrians (732 BCE) and the Jewish resettling of the Galilee by the Hasmoneans, it is impossible to define any borders."[12] He later discusses that this is due in part to the lack of settlement in the area in general. He notes that "archaeological surveys in the Galilee have not demonstrated almost any continuation of settlements between the eighth and fifth centuries BCE."[13] Gal concurs, noting that:

> I conclude that the entire northern part of the kingdom of Israel was devastated, and the Assyrian source focused on the southern part of

Lower Galilee, namely Zebulun. This hypothesis is positively supported by the results of archaeological survey. It appears as if Lower
Galilee was significantly deserted and its inhabitants exiled to Assur.
Moreover, according to the historical sources as well as the archaeological evidence, no new settlers were brought into the region as was
done later in Samaria. . . . [T]he region was not occupied during the
seventh and sixth centuries B.C.E.[14]

Gal says that no resettlement begins until the mid-sixth century
BCE when Persian settlements are established in sites along the
coastal plain. New sites then appear in the Galilee shortly thereafter
representing the expansion into the rural hinterland from these re-
established urban centers. He notes: "It was a new beginning in the
history of Lower Galilee with numerous sites established and occupied for the first time."[15] Aviam agrees, "In my opinion, the Jewish
survivors [of the Assyrian conquest] gradually concentrated in the
western part of Lower Galilee." He cites Judith 1:8 as confirmation
of this observation, noting that Upper Galilee and the Jezreel Valley
are included in the list of gentile areas, but the Lower Galilee is not
mentioned at all. His supposition is that this is where the residual
Jewish population was domiciled.

In chapter 4, I will outline Bethsaida's establishment during the
later stages of this expansion, sometime during the fourth century
BCE. In any event, it becomes clear that one cannot understand the
Galilee as an area that remained unchanged from the First Temple
through the Second Temple periods. In fact, the evidence would
suggest that there is in fact no continuity of culture between the
two periods. As Jonathan Reed observes, "There is simply an in-
sufficient amount of material culture in the Galilee from after the
campaigns of Tiglath-Pileser III to consider seriously any cultural
continuity between earlier and subsequent centuries—there are no
villages, no hamlets, no farmsteads, nothing at all indicative of a
population that could harvest the Galilean valleys for the Assyrian
stores, much less sustain cultural and religious traditions through
the centuries."[16] However, Frankel seems to suggest that there is a
significant continuity of culture since twenty-eight of thirty-six of

his surveyed Iron II sites remain occupied. He further supports his claim by noting that, although much reduced in number, the settlement pattern of the Persian period is similar to that of Iron II. In fact he states there were new settlements in the Mount Meron area and previously abandoned Iron I sites are also reoccupied. Yet it is admitted that the status of Galilee is not mentioned in contemporary documents.[17] Therefore, the assumption of cultural continuity or of Assyrian presence may be just that, an assumption based on earlier administrative policies. It may be better to argue for a discontinuous resettlement that may have occurred following the widespread depopulation due to the Assyrian conquest.

Therefore, the reason for Bethsaida's nonappearance on maps is likely two-fold and not merely based upon a changing understanding of the borders of Galilee. First, the site of Et-Tell/Bethsaida was largely unexcavated and unpublished during the formulation of many of the projects surveying Galilee during the 1980s and early 1990s. For example, Bethsaida does not appear in Mordechai Aviam's work published in 2004, but largely consisting of articles of his work during the 1980s and 1990s.[18] Nor does it appear in David Adan-Bayewitz's study on Roman pottery from 1993, which was based on his doctoral work in the 1980s.[19]

Subsequent to this time period, though, an extensive program of excavation and survey in the Galilee and Golan has vastly expanded the knowledge of Galilee in antiquity. Beginning in the 1980s these excavations and surveys have uncovered material cultural remains that illustrate important aspects of life in the region during the Hellenistic, Roman, and Byzantine periods. This archaeological activity has included the entire gamut from urban material culture to rural, elite to common, pagan to Jewish.[20] More recently Bethsaida has begun to be included in the data collections. For example, Bethsaida does appear in Jonathan Reed's recent work[21]

The second reason for the "nonappearance" of Bethsaida in the past has been the fact that Bethsaida had ceased to be an inhabited location before the advent of Byzantine Christianity in the region. Thus in late antiquity, it largely disappears from the discussion of Jewish/Christian relations.

Nonetheless, Bethsaida cannot be understood apart from a larger understanding of the Galilee. Therefore, we begin our exploration of the relationship between Bethsaida and the understanding of the setting for Galilean Christianity by surveying the various perspectives brought to bear upon the region.

Indeed, we need to begin by discussing the origin of the name, Galilee, itself.

GALILEE OF THE GENTILES

The Hebrew word גליל, translated Galilee, derives from the root גלל meaning "to roll" and was translated as "circle" or "district."[22] The feminine form, גלילה, refers to a region or district, and it was applied to several regions including regions in Philistia and along the Jordan. The term occurs in Joshua 20:7[23] where the cities of refuge are mentioned: ויקדשו את־קדש בגליל בהר נפתלי ואת־שכם בהר אפרים ואת־קרית ארבע היא חברון בהר יהודה: (They set apart Kadesh in Galilee in the hill country of Naphtali, Shechem in the hill country of Ephraim and Kiryat Arbeh, which is Hebron, in the hill country of Judah.). Kadesh in Galilee is again mentioned in Joshua 21:32, and 1 Chronicles 6:67.[24] The expression "land of Galilee," בארץ הגליל occurs in I Kings 9:11 where Solomon gives King Hiram 20 cities in the region in payment for services rendered in the building program of his kingdom. Upon inspection Hiram politely suggests that they are not much— ארץ כבול (9:13).

The name may also appear in the town list of Thutmoses III. R. Frankel suggests that an entry, *k-r-r*, on the late Bronze Age list is to be read as Galilee.[25] This along with the six biblical references that refer to the Galilee suggests that Galilee most certainly coincided with the northern mountain region of Naphtali that was encircled by valleys.

The identification of the inhabitants of Galilee during the Hellenistic-Roman period has often centered upon an interpretation of the meaning of the much earlier text, Isaiah 8:23/9:1. The traditional interpretation of *galil haggoyim* גליל הגוים has been taken to mean that the region was populated by non-Israelites in the aftermath of the Assyrian conquest, which depopulated the region. But, as we have seen above, this does not match the archaeological evidence for the Iron Age Galilee.

1 Macc 5:15 echoes the phrase with γαλιλαια αλοφυλων[26] and so it is further assumed that in the early Hellenistic times reflected in the Maccabean literature the region was still occupied by non-Jews with only a minority Jewish presence. Thus, the epithet "Galilee of the Gentiles" has been regarded as a descriptive term beyond what may have been a geographic locative. The phrase "Galilee of the Gentiles" often carries connotations concerning the ethnic make-up, cultural sophistication, and religious orientation of the populace. Indeed, some scholars have debated whether or not the shorter term "Galilee" is not simply an abbreviation of the longer "Galilee of the Gentiles." The "of the peoples (gentiles)" may be a later explanatory addition.[27]

One may even wonder if the Jewish/gentile dichotomy is not mixed with the Greek/barbarian dichotomy to produce the interesting stereotype of Galilean Jews as being seen as bucolic ruffians as in, for example, the Petrine denial pericopes where Peter is recognized as a Galilean (Mk 14:70 and parallels) or the Acts account of Pentecost where the bystanders remark in amazement at the linguistic prowess of the apostles, "Are not all these who are speaking Galileans?" (Acts 2:7).[28]

Sean Freyne in his *Anchor Bible* article on Galileans points out the implications of using this epithet as a starting point in reconstructing the conditions of first century Galilee:

> If, for example, the Galileans of the 1st century B.C.E. were largely forced converts to Judaism, would that fact influence our perception of their religious laxity when judged by the standards of later Jerusalem orthodoxy? If Galileans lived in conditions of social and economic deprivation, would this predispose us to view them as apocalyptically motivated revolutionaries?[29]

In contrast to this interpretative stereotyping, however, one need note that the region was included in the territory of an ethnarch

within the Roman administration. It was recognized as Jewish territory by Pompey in that he assigned the region to the ethnarch John
Hyrcanus.[30]

HELLENISM AND THE GALILEE

One sees then that reconstructions of first century Galilee from the
literary sources often lead to a misconstrued conception of the population of the region. The understanding of origins and make-up of
the people inhabiting the Galilee are in many cases patently wrong
because of the notion of a repopulated Galilee begun by Assyrian
(i.e., non-Jewish) colonists. This then leads to further assumptions
of the make-up of the population in later periods and their openness
to the pagan influences of Hellenistic culture, but does not draw on
any significant sources for the later (post-Assyrian) make-up of the
population. One cannot assume that there were no changes.

The popular view of the Galilee region of the late Hellenistic/
early Roman period can perhaps best be summarized by using the
words of John P. Meier: "Greek culture and language made increasing inroads in Palestine."[31] In his reconstruction of the period,
Greek culture spread from the hubs of Greek language and culture,
mainly the urban centers, founded by the Seleucids. His estimation
is that the degree of Hellenization "certainly was massive."[32] However, the precise degree and form it locally took was left somewhat
ambiguous.

Yet, to understand Galilee only in terms of its ethnic or cultural
identity, between what is "Jewish" or "Hellenistic," is to reduce the
complexity of relationship between the dual partners in the composition of Hellenism. Hellenism is a composite of both its Greek and
indigenous sources. It is perhaps a mistake to think in terms of an
ability to clearly distinguish boundaries around what is Jewish (that
is, distinctly non-Hellenistic) and what is "Hellenistic" (that is, what
is distinctly non–Near Eastern). It is more useful to think in terms
of a fluidity of negotiation between many different influences, ex-
pressions, and identities. There is therefore no monolithic expres-

sion of either Judaism or of Hellenism present in any given place/ time. In fact, the two cultural foci, Jewish and non-Jewish (gentile), are not even to be thought of in terms of indigenous and foreign, but instead both should be placed within an emerging form of Hellenism. We should not consider the whole process of Hellenization as forcibly imposed, necessarily, but instead it may be seen "rather as a cultural force that enabled indigenous cultures, both Jewish and gentile, to express themselves better and just as authentically."[33]

F. E. Peters speaks of two modes of Hellenism, a gentle and an assertive Hellenism. He describes the Hellenization of the Jews as a competition of ideals, the polis, and the Mosaic law.[34] He seems to divide the types of Hellenism according to the political power at home in Judea and the Galilee. The Ptolemies were purveyors of the "gentle" Hellenism that was influenced by prosperity, a moneyed economy, and spiritualization by means of an intellectualist ethic. There was lacking in this "gentle" form of Hellenism any direct challenge to participation by the Jewish community that required a choosing between participation in the rites of the polis/oikumene and observance of the Mosaic Law. This view is consistent with what Eric Meyers later posits: "The appearance of some forms of Greco-Roman culture need not signify compromise, accommodation or traumatic change but simply a way of expressing local culture in new and often exciting ways."[35]

All of that changed, according to Peters, with the emerging dominance of the Seleucid empire over the region. The Seleucids sought to enforce participation in the life of the imperial culture. Peters raises the interesting distinction between political Hellenism and cultural Hellenism. Richard Horsley recognizes this distinction as well. He states: "It is therefore unlikely that much of historical significance will be generated by applying the opposition of 'Hellenistic versus Jewish' to Galilee in early Roman times apart from the political-economic relations between the people concerned."[36] Therefore, following this line of reasoning, while political Hellenism may be undeniably "massive," it does not necessarily follow that the infiltration or adoption of cultural Hellenism was progressing as rapidly. Nor does it follow that the subsequent confrontations, as recounted in the intertestamental literature of the Maccabees, reflect solely an irreconcilable disjunction between Hellenism and Jewishness. The Seleucids focused on the enforced participation in the cultus that was part of the Seleucid understanding of the polis and empire as a basis of organization for social life, not necessarily on cultural Hellenism.

Shaye Cohen amplifies this concept of cultural Hellenism. He notes that, like the Jews, the Hellenes also had a conceptual idea of cultural distinctiveness. The world was divided by the Hellenes between Greeks and barbarians, similar to the Jewish division of Jew and gentile. However, the contours of the boundary, which are never clearly drawn for either group, are nevertheless more easily crossed by the barbarian than the gentile. In this case, "polytheism was tolerant, monotheism was not."[37] One need only add Greek language and participation in the polis to become "civilized." This was not possible with the monotheistic faith of the Mosaic Jewish community that required a relinquishing of all competing religious claims. One could perhaps speak Greek and be observant, but one could not participate in the cult of the polis and remain within the observant community.[38]

However, that distinction is clearly not resolved for those who claim that gentiles and/or Hellenic Jews were numerous in the Galilee of Jesus, which is a common perspective in New Testament scholarship. Most encyclopedic sources claim that gentiles are a large and highly visible component of the total population of the area.[39]

This gentile presence is equated with the presence of Hellenism. One should consider though what is meant by Hellenism. Hellenism is defined by Shaye Cohen in two ways. For the typical view of widespread gentile presence in Hellenistic Galilee, only his first definition is seemingly applicable. "'Hellenism' means the culture, society, and way of life brought to the peoples of the east by Alexander the Great and his successors."[40] Therefore, to call a culture Hellenistic implies that its language, literature, ideas, gods, and social elite were Greek and that the dominant form of social organization was the polis. One can see from this definition that this Hellenism is then antithetical to Judaism. Cohen notes that First and Second Maccabees certainly understood things this way because in 2 Maccabees[41] the terms Judaism and Hellenism are employed as antonyms.[42] Under this contrastive definition of Hellenism, Hellenistic Jews of the Diaspora were seen as guilty of adulterating their Jewishness by employing the Greek language and importing Greek ideas and practices into their practice of Judaism. The use of the phrase "Galilee of the Gentiles," then, reflects this worldview, a Jewish minority struggling to observe their religion in a hostile context. Richard Horsley also observes this phenomenon in the current scholarly paradigm when he states that although it is a somewhat more nuanced and qualified understanding, it still amounts to a contrastive relationship: "'Judaism/Jewish' is [. . .] counterpoised with 'Hellenism/Hellenistic.'"[43]

However, Cohen argues that Hellenism is more correctly understood as the fusion of Greek and local culture and not the dichotomous polarity of the two. All Jewish culture would be part of Hellenism under this definition, just as Hellenism was in part formed from Judaism. That is, there was influence between the two former culturally distinct entities of Greek culture, on the one hand, and post-exilic Judaism, on the other. The fusion did not result in the former entities being present in the new construction in equal measure, however. As Cohen notes, the Hellenistic world was manifested in a common material culture, language, and life pathway. To what degree one was integrated into this world was debatable, but not whether or not one would be a part.

Richard Horsley would frame the distinction in terms of an urban/rural issue. In doing so, according to Halvor Moxnes, Horsley "presents Jesus as a renewer and defender of traditional village life in Galilee against the power of the elite."[44] (For elite one could read "gentiles" or Hellenistic Jewish overlords.) He casts the relationships in terms of the power dynamics between the urban areas and rural hinterland. His picture of Galilee is a classical one of a region dominated by an imperial power, in this case imperial power through the reign of a client intermediary.[45]

Horsley is not alone in doing this, as Frédéric Manns notes:

Studies made by Scroggs and Clark are based generally on those of Meeks and Theissen. They put in contrast the world of the New Testament with the world of early Christianity. While Jesus preached in the rural milieu of Palestine, Paul rooted Christianity in the big Hellenistic cities.[46]

There are, however, three possible positions concerning the existence and the nature of Galilean urban-rural interaction and each is portrayed in the secondary literature.[47] The first denies any urban-rural relationship in Roman Galilee. That is, despite geographical proximity, urban and rural populations remain stringently separated. E. P. Sanders, representative of this first position, states that the urban and rural populations would never have interacted for "[i]n real life, the peasants worked from dawn to dusk six days a week and rested on the Sabbath [and] for holidays they went to Jerusalem."[48] Sanders, as is clear, presupposes that the urban centers were Hellenized and that the surrounding countryside was not. Thus, the peasantry would not have ventured into Hellenized urban centers even if their workload, Sabbath observance, and cultic relationship with Jerusalem had not precluded urban-rural interaction. Indeed, "[p]aganism up close would have scared them or offended them."[49]

The second position allows for urban-rural interaction in the Galilee but argues that the form that this interaction took was one of animosity. This, as we have seen, is the position taken by Horsley. Often this urban-rural animosity is seen as part of the general class hostility. The elite landlords resided in the urban centers while their rural peasant tenants lived in the countryside.[50] Shimon Applebaum cites y. Hor. III, 48c as evidence of urban-rural antagonism in the Galilee in the last decades of the second century CE and describes the basic antagonism as "originat[ing] in what the landlord took from his tenant or his debtor, and in the power which he accumulated thereby."[51]

Jonathan Reed takes a similar position. He states that urban-rural contact was not uncommon and suggests several means through which rural Galileans acquired first-hand or second-hand knowledge of Sepphoris and Tiberias, "whether as agricultural suppliers or, less likely, through commercial contacts; perhaps to visit family and clan members who had moved there; or to visit the market, solicit services, or be hauled before court."[52] From his perspective the urban-rural relationship was one of enmity because of the economic strain that these cities created in rural areas.

Freyne likewise describes the urban-rural relationship to be one of antagonism. However, he states that "to suggest that the relationship between the Galilean *ek tes choras*[53] and these cities was uniformly hostile is a generalization and ignores particular circumstances operative in individual instances."[54] Yet, he goes on to hold that "rural animosities toward the cities were deep-seated and permanent."[55] His argument is based on the distinction made by Redfield and Singer between the orthogenic role of the city, that is, "the carrying forward into systematic and reflective dimensions of an old culture," and the heterogenic role of the city, that is, "the creating of original modes of thought that have authority beyond or in conflict with old cultures and civilizations."[56] He goes on to distinguish a refinement to Redfield and Singer that he calls primary and secondary urbanization. This distinction focuses on the relationship between the urban center and the surrounding folk culture. Primary urbanization is a kind of indigenous urbanization whereby the urban center coalesces the surrounding folk culture tradition into a Tradition. Secondary urbanization is an imposed cultural center that is placed in a divergent folk, peasant, or semi-urban culture by means of expansion or conquest.[57] Using the writings of Josephus and the Gospels as his sources, Freyne argues that the urban-rural relationship of mistrust and hostility originated from the orthogenic orientation of the rural population and the heterogenic orientation of the urban population. Also, he argues that the Hellenistic urbanization imposed by the ruling Ptolemies, Seleucids, or Romans was secondary in nature.

In a separate article, Freyne identifies debt as another factor contributing to urban-rural animosity. He noted that this peasant debt was a "direct result of the elites drawing off the resources of the countryside, but without any productive reinvestment."[58] He finds in *Life* 375–76 evidence of "a peasantry frustrated with centers which were not prepared to offer the kind of solidarity between town and country that might have been expected but which was not in fact forthcoming."[59] Thus, for Freyne, urban-rural animosity was a function of both the conflicting value systems of the rural and urban areas and peasant debt.

The third position holds that a cooperative urban-rural interaction occurred in the Galilee. This position arises from a survey of the archaeological evidence that confirms that intra-regional trade of manufactured goods occurred in Roman Galilee. Recent studies of pottery using neutron activation analysis, as a supplement to observational typology, found that artifacts, consisting mainly of common kitchen ware and storage jars, that were recovered in Galilean excavations were originally manufactured in the villages of Kefar Hananya and Shihin.[60] Based on the absence of literary references to the manufacturing of pottery in either Sepphoris or Tiberias and on the fact that the pottery of Kefar Hananya and Shihin accounted for the bulk of the household pottery used in Roman Sepphoris, Adan-Bayewitz concludes that the Galilean cities, particularly of Sepphoris and Tiberias, had been dependent upon these rural settlements to supply various manufactured products.[61] Conversely, Sepphoris is seen as a distribution center of the locally manufactured pottery.[62] Thus, Adan-Bayewitz concludes that a cooperative relationship existed between Kefar Hananya and Sepphoris because of their interdependence.

Douglas E. Oakman, however, discerns a need for an explicit systems model in this interpretation of pottery distribution.[63] He states that archaeology needs to distinguish between cultural and social indices. A cultural index is a reflection of a "prevalent value" of a people that may be shared across economic and social lines. For first century Judaism this would include such phenomena as aniconic coins. A social index implies something is reflected in the material culture that is introduced because of inequities of power and wealth.[64] Therefore, arguing solely from the distribution pattern of the pottery in and of itself, allows for a range of possible explanations. Oakman points out two relevant issues. First, for example, the elite in Sepphoris could have owned the pottery manufacturing workshops in the villages, or controlled the trade through licensure and taxation, or, as Adan-Bayewitz argues, there could indeed have been a mutually equitable relationship. To assume distribution center equals a "market relationship" is, according to Oakman, to misunderstand ancient markets.[65] Second, Oakman suggests that one "might ask whether other pottery manufacturing outlets [or supplies] could have existed *de jure* (given the necessary supplies of local clay), but did not *de facto* because of the prevailing sociopolitical arrangements."[66] That is, Oakman cautions that one may miss "non-elite social action" if one ignores social systems theory that help us explore the interaction between elites and non-elites in the first century.[67]

Douglas Edwards, in his assessment of the socioeconomic status of the Galilee in the first century CE, notes that the gospels show this cooperative commercial interaction between the urban and rural areas in their depiction of the movement of Jesus and the disciples. He illustrates this with findings from important survey studies of the Galilee.[68] Edwards notes that Eric Meyers has previously called attention to the fact that the four valleys that traverse the Lower Galilee provided natural avenues for trade from the east to the coast.[69] Edwards further highlights the fact that Magen Broshi extends the significance of this economic prime requisite for urban development in antiquity with his observation that the population density of the entire Lower Galilee region in late antiquity was one of the highest in the whole Roman empire.[70]

In short, three positions are present in secondary literature concerning the occurrence and nature of urban-rural interaction in Roman Galilee. The first position finds the urban-rural relationship to be nonexistent in Roman Galilee because of Hellenism; the second position finds the style of interaction to be one of animosity, again as a result of Hellenism among other factors; and the third finds the interaction to reflect amicable reciprocity, in this case because the culture is shared to an extent that allows easy interaction between urban and rural settings.

Mark A. Chancey notes another important distinction in the role and relation of Hellenism and local culture. According to him, one should distinguish between Hellenism and paganism rather than use the two synonymously.[71] Just as there is political and cultural Hellenism, so is there, in a sense, religious and secular Hellenism. For Chancey, Hellenism is the presence of Greco-Roman culture whereas paganism is the worship of any deity other than the Jewish god. As he states, "The presence of Hellenism at a site does not necessarily indicate the presence of pagans, and the presence of pagans does not necessarily indicate the presence of Hellenism."[72] For example, Aviam notes that at Kafar Yasif, located near Acco, a Greek inscription dedicated to Hadad and Atargatis was found. This obviously is pagan, but non-Greek, that is pagan from a Near Eastern background and not a Hellenic origin and so may be indicative of pagan influence but not necessarily that of Hellenism, other than in the use of Greek language.[73]

Likewise one can cite, although from a later period, that many synagogues have lintel inscriptions in Greek and even make use of zodiacal mosaic floors, although these structures are obviously not used in pagan worship. This may become an important distinction to consider when evaluating the use of language, images, and motifs from the larger cultural context. That is, a Hellenistic laden object found in a Jewish context need not be indicative of a "gentile presence." Prof. Larry Schiffman uses a helpful illustration in speaking about how some objects may be found "innocently" in a context. He mentions that the synagogue he attends serves cola in a Santa Claus can during the holiday season, but that is not an indication of the practice of the associated Christmas rituals of Santa. It is merely the culturally available container at the time. Schiffman adds, "Even Jews who were loyal Jews may have been a bit loose on some of the decorations that they had, sort of like the Santa Claus on Coca Cola that is served in my synagogue every winter, but this doesn't really mean that anybody was even religiously attached to that."[74]

Eric Meyers states a similar point of view:

> It is my view that despite the urbanization policies of Rome the Galilee remained predominantly Jewish throughout the Roman period, especially in the first century. It is simply not accurate any longer to argue

for a Hellenistic or cosmopolitan character to the Galilee on the basis of presumptions about the demographic makeup of a particular city or region. . . . Even the more frequent appearance of Hellenistic features at sites such as Sepphoris with temple, theater, villa, etc., does not necessarily point to a greater accommodation to gentile or pagan culture.[75]

Meyers would suggest that there was symbiosis and not confrontation between Hellenism and the Jewish community. Thus, one should not equate paganism and Hellenism.

A FOCUS ON GALILEE

The Historical Jesus movement has added to this Galilee of the Gentiles perspective. Although the focus of the interest in Galilee has shifted from the earlier pre-twentieth century quest of the historical Jesus, or even the earlier forms of that quest, nonetheless the interest in reconstructing the Galilee to understand Jesus continues. The perspective may have moved from a quest for the psychological impact of the region on the formation of Jesus to a more communal sense that sees not the relationship between geography and character but the complex of relationships between geography, inhabitants, and power as providing the cultural, political, economic, and social structure for identity formation.

Two factors had seemingly remained constant until recently, however. One was the understanding of the possibility and, in fact, desirability of producing an accurate representation of the ancient world. The other was the understanding of geography, namely, that the landscape creates, shapes, or dominates that form of human culture which develops. That is, "topos and physis is what shapes, what gives form and content to nomos and ethos."[76]

A new sense of Galilee as a "place," a mindscape of cultural geography, is replacing the older understanding.[77] James Strange notes regarding Josephus' understanding of the Galilee:

Although hills, valleys, and soils may have been of interest to many in his audience, they did not occupy him, nor will they detain us. Rather our overall goal is to capture a snapshot, as it were, of the metaphorical map of Sepphoris and Galilee that appears to underlie the prose of the *Vita*. I will argue that Josephus in the *Vita* uses Sepphoris (and Tiberias) as a kind of metaphorical marker in an imaginative map of Galilee. He is not so much interested in a literal map as in engendering a mental map in his readers. This map is mostly comprised of two major cities, Sepphoris and Tiberias, with some excursions to Gabara and Taricheae, and several other villages and towns.[78]

Thus, the new geographical understanding of the Galilee is, in fact, already present in the ancient literature. By extension, then, even the biblical material should perhaps be seen as metaphorical "mindscape" or "theoscape," setting a stage for a cognitive understanding of the perspective of the author rather than an objective sense of "real" place. Halvor Moxnes notes that "Galilee has become a spatial metaphor for Hellenism understood as culture in socio-intellectual terms."[79] It is the modern spatial metaphor that we wish to address by introducing the cultural material uncovered at Bethsaida. The modern construct must take into account the actual archaeological remains of the Galilee.

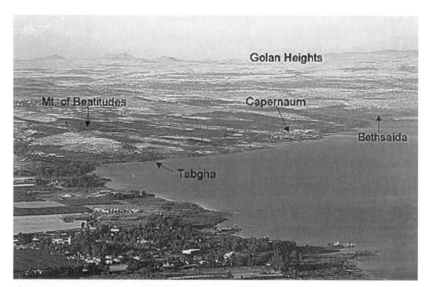

Figure 2.1.   Photograph of Northern Sea of Galilee
Source: www.bibleplaces.com

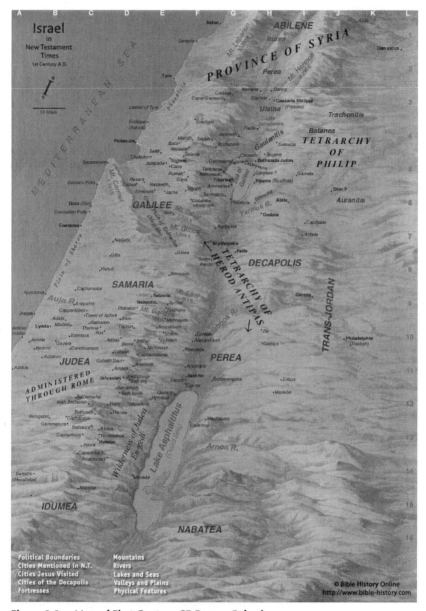

Figure 2.2.   Map of First Century CE Roman Palestine
Source: Bible History Online, www.bible-history.com

Figure 2.3. Map of Galilee and Northern Palestine
Source: Author adapted from Bible History Online map of Galilee and Northern Palestine

NOTES

1. John Wesley, *Explanatory Notes Upon the New Testament* (Grand Rapids, MI: Baker Book House, 1745, reprint 1981), note Matthew 4:15.

2. H. W. Wilson, "Galilee," *A Guide to the Ancient World* (1986), www.credoreference.com/entry/5073300 (accessed August 13, 2007).

3. They came to Philip, who was from Bethsaida in Galilee, with a request. "Sir," they said, "we would like to see Jesus." John 12:21 NIV.

4. Jack Finegan, *Light from the Ancient Past the Archeological Background of Judaism and Christianity* (Princeton, NJ: Princeton University Press, 1959), 307.

5. In Geographia 5.16.4, Ptolemy refers to Bethsaida as Julias, the name Philip gave the city when he gave it polis status.

6. Strange, *Sepphoris and Galilee in Josephus' Vita*, 2.

7. Sean Freyne, *Galilee, from Alexander the Great to Hadrian, 323 B.C.E. to 135 C.E. a Study of Second Temple Judaism* (Wilmington, DE, and Notre Dame, IN: M. Glazier University of Notre Dame Press, 1980), 9.

8. Zvi Gal, *Lower Galilee during the Iron Age* (Winona Lake, IN: Eisenbrauns, 1992), 1.

9. Salomon E. Grootkerk, *Ancient Sites in Galilee: A Toponymic Gazetteer*, Culture and History of the Ancient Near East (Leiden and Boston: Brill, 2000), 248–49, map 20. It is interesting to note that Grootkerk has a remark that the site was of "mixed population" during the classical period, which he defines as 330 BC to 640 AD.

10. Leonard Elliott-Binns, *Galilean Christianity* (Chicago: A. R. Allenson, 1956), 15.

11. He concludes that Luke's insertion of Bethsaida into the narrative at 9:1ff. is indicative of his "ignorance of the country." Elliott-Binns, *Galilean Christianity*, 30.

12. Mordechai Aviam, *Jews, Pagans, and Christians in the Galilee: 25 Years of Archaeological Excavations and Surveys: Hellenistic to Byzantine Periods* (Rochester, NY: University of Rochester Press, 2004), 11.

13. Aviam, *Jews, Pagans, and Christians in the Galilee: 25 Years of Archaeological Excavations and Surveys: Hellenistic to Byzantine Periods*, 41.

14. Gal, *Lower Galilee During the Iron Age*, 108.

15. Aviam, *Jews, Pagans, and Christians in the Galilee: 25 Years of Archaeological Excavations and Surveys: Hellenistic to Byzantine Periods*, 109.

16. Jonathan L. Reed, "Galileans, 'Israelite Village Communities,' and the Sayings Gospel Q," in *Galilee Through the Centuries: Confluence of Cultures*, ed. Eric M. Meyers, Duke Judaic Studies Series (Winona Lake, IN: Eisenbrauns, 1999), 93.

17. Rafi Frankel, *Settlement Dynamics and Regional Diversity in Ancient Upper Galilee: Archaeological Survey of Upper Galilee*, IAA Reports (Jerusalem: Israel Antiquities Authority, 2001), 107.

18. Aviam, *Jews, Pagans, and Christians in the Galilee: 25 Years of Archaeological Excavations and Surveys: Hellenistic to Byzantine Periods*.

19. David Adan-Bayewitz, *Common Pottery in Roman Galilee: A Study of Local Trade*, Bar-Ilan Studies in Near Eastern Languages and Culture (Ramat-Gan, Israel: Bar-Ilan University Press, 1993).

20. See for example Sharon C. Herbert and Donald T. Ariel, *Tel Anafa I: Final Report on Ten Years of Excavation at a Hellenistic and Roman Settlement in Northern Israel*, Journal of Roman Archaeology (Ann Arbor, MI: Kelsey Museum of the University of Michigan, 1994) for a "pagan/urban" site, or Shemaryah Gutman, *Gamla Ha-Hafirot Bi-Shemoneh Ha- Onot Ha-Rishonah* (Tel-Aviv: Hotsa at ha-Kibuts ha-me uhad, 1981) for a "Jewish/ urban" site.

21. Reed, *Archaeology and the Galilean Jesus: A Re-Examination of the Evidence*.

22. It is interesting to note that even in the dictionary entry there is the notation in heading 2 that states "population largely heathen." Francis Brown, et al., *The Brown-Driver-Briggs Hebrew and English Lexicon with an Appendix Containing the Biblical Aramaic: Coded with the Numbering System from Strong's Exhaustive Concordance of the Bible* (Peabody, MA: Hendrickson Publishers, 1996), 165.

23. In some English translations, Galilee also appears in Joshua 12:23. However, the Hebrew has גלגל and not גליל. The English translation follows the LXX source for the verse: βασιλεα Γει τνς Γαλιλαιας.

24. In the topographical name lists of Thutmoses III located in the temple of Amon at Karnak there are listed two pertinent names. The first name in the Palestine list is Qadesh (q-d-s). Jan Jozef Simons, *Handbook for the Study of Egyptian Topographical Lists Relating to Western Asia* (Leiden: E. J. Brill, 1937), 35, 111, 115.

25. Frankel, *Settlement Dynamics and Regional Diversity in Ancient Upper Galilee: Archaeological Survey of Upper Galilee*, 141. He cites Simons 1937 work List 1, No. 80: Simons, *Handbook for the Study of Egyptian Topographical Lists Relating to Western Asia*, 112, translation and note on 118.

26. Jonathan Goldstein notes in his commentary on 1 Maccabees that the translator renders the Hebrew גוים with a Greek word used in the LXX to translate Philistines, normally indicating "foreigners." Jonathan A. Goldstein, *I Maccabees: A New Translation, with Introduction and Commentary*, Anchor Bible (Garden City, NY: Doubleday, 1976), 299.

27. Frankel, *Settlement Dynamics and Regional Diversity in Ancient Upper Galilee: Archaeological Survey of Upper Galilee*, 142.

28. Robert W. Wall, "The Acts of The Apostles," in *The New Interpreter's Bible, Volume X* (Nashville: Abingdon, 2002), 55. Wall notes that Galileans

were "notorious for their lack of linguistic talent." But the source for this notoriety is not given.

29. Sean Freyne, "Galileans," in *Anchor Bible Dictionary Volume 2* (New York: Doubleday, 1992), 877.

30. Sean Freyne, "Hellenistic/Roman Galilee," in *Anchor Bible Dictionary Volume 2* (New York: Doubleday, 1992), 898.

31. Meier, *A Marginal Jew: Rethinking the Historical Jesus*, 258.

32. Meier, *A Marginal Jew: Rethinking the Historical Jesus*, 258.

33. Eric M. Meyers, "Jesus and His Galilean Context," in *Archaeology and the Galilee: Texts and Contexts in the Graeco-Roman and Byzantine Periods* (Atlanta, GA: Scholars Press, 1997), 64.

34. F. E. Peters, *The Harvest of Hellenism a History of the Near East from Alexander the Great to the Triumph of Christianity* (New York: Simon and Schuster, 1971), 261ff.

35. Meyers, "Jesus and His Galilean Context," 64.

36. Horsley, *Galilee History, Politics, People*, 7.

37. Cohen, *From the Maccabees to the Mishnah*, 35.

38. There may be, however, evidence that even this participation in veneration of the state was adapted to a form that could reside within the Jewish community. A "Jewish alternative" provided that the religious aspects of veneration were performed by means acceptable to the religious proprieties of the Jewish practices. Certainly prayers, tribute, and perhaps even some form of sacrifice could be performed in venerating the state leader. See David Golinkin, "Prayers for the Government," *Insight Israel* 6, no. 9 (May 2006) for a good brief overview on the subject.

39. For example, Mark Chancey notes in his survey that many scholars follow this notion of the nature of the Galilee: "See also F. C. Grant, 'Jesus Christ,' in Buttrick et al., eds., *Interpreter's Dictionary of the Bible*, Vol. II, 869–96; W. R. F. Browning, 'Galilee,' in W. R. F. Browning, ed., *A Dictionary of the Bible* (Oxford and New York: Oxford University Press, 1996), 145; Arthur M. Ross, 'Galilee,' in J. D. Douglas, Merrill C. Tenney et al., eds., *The New International Dictionary: Pictorial Edition* (Grand Rapids, MI: Zondervan Publishing House; Basingstoke, UK: Marshall Pickering, 1987), 368–69; Henry W. Holloman, 'Galilee, Galileans,' in Walter A. Elwell et al., eds., *Baker Encyclopedia of the Bible*, 2 vols. (Grand Rapids, MI: Baker Book House, 1986), vol. I, 834–836; no author, 'Galilee,' in John L. McKenzie, ed., *Dictionary of the Bible* (Milwaukee: Bruce Publishing Company, 1965), 293–294; R. W. Stewart MacAlister and Emil G. Kraeling, 'Galilee,' in James Hastings, Frederick C. Grant, and H. H. Rowley, eds.,

Dictionary of the Bible (New York: Charles Scribner's Sons, 1963), 313–314; 'Galilee,' in John E. Steinmueller and Kathryn Sullivan, eds., *Catholic Biblical Encyclopedia: New Testament* (New York: Joseph F. Wagner, Inc.: 1950), 248–249; 'Galilee,' in Herbert Lockyer et al., eds., *Nelson's Illustrated Bible Dictionary* (Nashville: Thomas Nelson Publishers, 1986), 401–402. The three most recent reference articles avoid this view, however; see Sean Freyne, 'Galilee,' in *OEANE*, vol. II, 369–376; Sean Freyne, 'Galilee (Hellenistic/Roman),' in *ABD*, vol. II, 895–899; Mordechai Aviam, 'Galilee: The Hellenistic to Byzantine Periods,' *NEAEHL*, vol. II, 453–458." Chancey, *The Myth of a Gentile Galilee: The Population of Galilee and New Testament Studies*, 1 fn. 2. One may also include other older sources such as Wesley's Notes on the NT, etc. This has been the predominate view of the Galilee in Christian interpretation.

40. Cohen, *From the Maccabees to the Mishnah*, 35.

41. 2 Maccabees 4:13.

42. Cohen, *From the Maccabees to the Mishnah*, 35.

43. Horsley, *Galilee History, Politics, People*, 3.

44. Halvor Moxnes, "The Construction of Galilee as a Place for the Historical Jesus—Part II," *Biblical Theology Bulletin*, Summer 2001, 4.

45. Horsley discusses both the urban/rural interaction and the impact of imperial administration on life in the Galilee. See Horsley, *Galilee History, Politics, People*, 7–11.

46. Frédéric Manns, "A Survey of Recent Studies on Early Christianity," in *Early Christianity in Context Monuments and Documents*, ed. Frédéric Manns (Jerusalem: Franciscan Printing Press, 1993), 17.

47. The framework portraying these positions is taken from Agnes Choi, "The Traveling Peasant and Urban-Rural Relations in Roman Galilee," Canadian Society of Biblical Studies Seminar (University of Western Ontario, London, Ontario, 2005), www.philipharland.com/travel/TravelChoiGalilee .pdf (accessed August 23, 2007).

48. E. P. Sanders, "Jesus' Galilee," in *Fair Play Diversity and Conflicts in Early Christianity: Essays in Honour of Heikki Räisänen*, Supplements to Novum Testamentum (Leiden Boston: Brill, 2002), 38.

49. Sanders, "Jesus' Galilee," 38.

50. Shimon Applebaum, "Judaea as a Roman Province; the Countryside as a Political and Economic Factor," *Aufstieg und Niedergang der Römischen Welt (ANRW)* II, no. 8 (1977): 355–96.

51. Applebaum, "Judaea as a Roman Province; the Countryside as a Political and Economic Factor," 372–73.

52. Reed, *Archaeology and the Galilean Jesus: A Re-Examination of the Evidence*, 99.

53. Life 21, 102; 47, 242–44.

54. Sean Freyne, "Urban-Rural Relations in First-Century Galilee," in *The Galilee in Late Antiquity*, ed. Lee I. Levine (New York and Cambridge, MA: Jewish Theological Seminary of America distributed by Harvard University Press, 1992), 83.

55. Freyne, "Urban-Rural Relations in First-Century Galilee," 83.

56. Freyne, "Urban-Rural Relations in First-Century Galilee," 76. He refers to Redfield and Singer's work where they note that "in ancient civilizations the urban centers were usually political-religious or political-intellectual." Robert Redfield and Milton Singer, "The Cultural Role of Cities," in *Economic Development and Cultural Change* (Chicago: University of Chicago Press, 1954), 54. The city creates a "state of mind" that may be at odds with the "local culture." Redfield and Milton Singer, "The Cultural Role of Cities," 57.

57. Freyne, "Urban-Rural Relations in First-Century Galilee," 76–77.

58. Sean Freyne, "Jesus and the Urban Culture of Galilee," in *Text and Contexts Biblical Texts in Their Textual and Situational Contexts: Essays in Honor of Lars Hartman*, ed. Tord Fornberg (Oslo and Boston: Scandinavian University Press, 1995), 606. He cites Martin Goodman, "The First Jewish Revolt: Social Conflict and the Problem of Debt," *The Journal of Jewish Studies* 33 (1982): 417–27 for this observation.

59. Freyne, "Jesus and the Urban Culture of Galilee," 606.

60. Adan-Bayewitz, *Common Pottery in Roman Galilee: A Study of Local Trade*, 170.

61. Adan-Bayewitz, *Common Pottery in Roman Galilee: A Study of Local Trade*, 211–19.

62. Adan-Bayewitz, *Common Pottery in Roman Galilee: A Study of Local Trade*, 211–19.

63. Douglas E. Oakman, "The Archaeology of First-Century Galilee and the Social Interpretation of the Historical Jesus," in *Society of Biblical Literature Seminar Papers* (Missoula, MT: Scholars Press, 1994), 232.

64. Oakman, "The Archaeology of First-Century Galilee and the Social Interpretation of the Historical Jesus," 227–28.

65. Oakman, "The Archaeology of First-Century Galilee and the Social Interpretation of the Historical Jesus," 232.

66. Oakman, "The Archaeology of First-Century Galilee and the Social Interpretation of the Historical Jesus," 232.

67. Oakman, "The Archaeology of First-Century Galilee and the Social Interpretation of the Historical Jesus," 227.

68. Edwards mentions particularly the Meiron survey by Myers, Strange, and Groh: Eric M. Meyers, "Galilean Regionalism as a Factor in Historical Reconstruction," *Bulletin of the American Schools of Oriental Research* 221 (1976): 93–102. Douglas R. Edwards, "First Century Urban/Rural Relations in Lower Galilee: Exploring Archaeological and Literary Evidence," *Society of Biblical Literature Seminar Papers* 27 (1988): 171.

69. Edwards, "First Century Urban/Rural Relations in Lower Galilee: Exploring Archaeological and Literary Evidence," 171. Edwards is citing Meyers' study on Galilean regionalism: Meyers, "Galilean Regionalism as a Factor in Historical Reconstruction." Meyers has subsequently re-presented these ideas in later articles. See, for example, Eric M. Meyers, "Roman Sepphoris in Light of New Archaeological Evidence and Recent Research," in *The Galilee in Late Antiquity*, ed. Lee I. Levine (New York Cambridge, MA: Jewish Theological Seminary of America distributed by Harvard University Press, 1992), 321–38.

70. Magen Broshi, "The Role of the Temple in the Herodian Economy," *The Journal of Jewish Studies* 38, no. 1 (Spring 1987): 32.

71. Chancey, *The Myth of a Gentile Galilee: The Population of Galilee and New Testament Studies*, 7.

72. Chancey, *The Myth of a Gentile Galilee: The Population of Galilee and New Testament Studies*, 7.

73. Aviam, *Jews, Pagans, and Christians in the Galilee: 25 Years of Archaeological Excavations and Surveys: Hellenistic to Byzantine Periods*, 17. He cites Michael Avi-Yonah's article on the "Syrian Gods at Ptolemais-'Akko.'" Michael Avi-Yonah, "Syrian Gods at Ptolemais-Akko," *Israel Exploration Journal*, no. 9 (1959): 1–12.

74. From his interview in Kirk Wolfinger, *Ancient Refuge in the Holy Land*, Gary Hochman, NOVA (Nebraska Educational Telecommunications for WGBH/Boston, 2004).

75. Eric M. Meyers, "Aspects of Roman Sepphoris in the Light of Recent Archaeology," in *Aspects of Roman Sepphoris in the Light of Recent Archaeology*, ed. Frédéric Manns (Jerusalem: Franciscan Printing Press, 1993), 33.

76. Jonathan Z. Smith, *To Take Place: Toward Theory in Ritual*, Chicago Studies in the History of Judaism (Chicago: University of Chicago Press, 1987), 30–31.

77. See Sawicki, *Crossing Galilee: Architectures of Contact in the Occupied Land of Jesus*, 37, and Richard A. Batey, "Is Not This the Carpenter?" *New Testament Studies* 30, no. 2 (1984): 249–58.

78. Strange, *Sepphoris and Galilee in Josephus' Vita*, 1–2.

79. Moxnes, "The Construction of Galilee as a Place for the Historical Jesus—Part II," 2.

3

THE STATE OF THE LAND AND ITS INHABITANTS

One must begin one's investigation of first century CE Et-Tell/ Bethsaida long before that specific time period. This is due in part to the assumptions that are made by social historians concerning the ethnic and cultural heritage of the population present in the land during the first century and their relationship to the contemporary political structure under which they exist.

A brief overview of the general sequence of events that occurred in the region historically and archaeologically may therefore be useful. This sequencing, however, is approached with the caveat that there is no consensus among scholars for a precise delineation of archaeological periods in Palestine. Yet, differentiating between archaeological periods can be done on the bases of two approaches. Either there is a clear transition in the archaeological material, or a major historical event is recounted in the literature that indicates a significant time of social upheaval. Hopefully, one is able to tie together both bases of demarcating cultural transition so that a known historical event clearly correlates with an evident change in the material record.

The focus of this investigation is the transitions between the Iron Age II and Persian periods, between the Persian and the Hellenistic periods, and between the Hellenistic and the Early Roman periods.

The first two transitions set the stage for understanding the social matrix that existed prior to our primary interest, the first century CE at Bethsaida. The latter transition may help us to understand the social make-up uncovered at Bethsaida. In any case, the material culture recovered at Bethsaida allows us to comment on some of the claims that scholars make concerning the state of the land and its population during some crucial periods of development for the understanding of the first century in the area.

THE IRON II TO PERSIAN PERIOD TRANSITION

The Iron Age II period has generally been thought to encompass the tenth through early sixth centuries BCE. This corresponds to the time of the united and divided monarchy of the kingdoms of Israel and Judah. Israeli scholars agree with this general framework, but tend to include the time of the united monarchy within Iron II as well. Archaeologically, one can certainly make a case from the ceramics that the tenth century should be set apart from the earlier Iron I period. The appearance of distinctive red slip and burnished ware characterizes the entire Iron II. From the historical side, the coalescence of the tribal Israelites into a territorial monarchy is a significant transition from Iron I.[1] The same process occurs among other presumably tribal groups, such as Moab, Ammon, and Edom, as well. One can then further subdivide the Iron II period into Iron IIA and Iron IIB, dividing at about 925 BCE on the basis of the historical event of Shishak's invasion of Palestine. This invasion has a significant impact on the material record of the region. Amihai Mazar notes that Shishak's campaign resulted in a widespread destruction of numerous sites. This coupled with the political division of the united monarchy creates a rather clear change in the material corpus.[2]

The Iron Age can be further subdivided with Iron IIC following the Assyrian conquest of the northern kingdom of Israel in 722 BCE. Thus, Iron IIA corresponds to 1000–925 BCE marked by the coalescing of tribal groups into monarchies until the Egyptian invasion of the territory; Iron IIB 900–722 BCE marked by the united and divided kingdoms of Israel and Judah until the Assyrian conquest; and Iron IIC 722–586 BCE or 539 BCE, marked by the first exile of Judah (598 BCE) and the subsequent Babylonian destruction (586 BCE).[3] Some scholars continue the Iron Age, sometimes with the terminology of Iron III designating the Neo-Babylonian period (586–539 BCE)[4], until later with the rise of Persian power in the area (539 BCE). In 539 BCE the Persian period commences for most scholars because of the end of Babylonian power and the consolidation of Persian power and lasts until the conquest by Alexander the Great in 332 BCE.[5] However, the beginning of the period shows a continuation of Iron II pottery traditions and so a clear demarcation in the material record is not recoverable. The transition is one of a gradual supplanting of earlier pottery types by indigenous and distinct new imported forms (or local imitations of foreign types).[6]

Beginning with the Iron IIB transition, we examine the material record of the general region for indications of transition. Most notably, the settlement pattern shows a discernible hierarchical pattern consistent with the presence of two local capitals, one in the north, Samaria, and one in the south, Jerusalem. Following these major urban areas are a second tier of "royal cities" such as Megiddo and Lachish. Next there are tertiary and quaternary cites, each succeeding tier smaller in extent. Four-chamber gates begin to make their appearance as well as the stone-covered glacis. Significant fortification of the major cities is evident, although varied in construction technique. Solid, casement, inset-offset and other wall types are evident.[7] At Bethsaida we have an extensive Iron IIB wall system of solid walls, a stone glacis, and a four-chambered gate.[8] The house structure remains as before in the area: the four-room type is still the fundamental floor plan. Monumental architecture is found notably in the tripartite building form that now becomes widespread and in ashlar construction.

Ephraim Stern notes that the time period we are investigating for the first of these major transitions in the population and material culture of the Bethsaida region is the time of the conquest of most of Palestine by the Assyrians. He proposes three major stages for this process extending over a period of nearly one hundred years: 1) the penetration, destruction and deportation of the Golan, Geshur (where Bethsaida is located), Philistia and the Israelite kingdom; 2) the consolidation of the conquest of Philistia and the destruction and conquest of most of Judah; 3) the campaign against Egypt.[9] It was during the first phase of the Assyrian campaigns in the entire region of Galilee that there was a generalized destruction of settlements. All major excavations note this destruction in their reports and many indicate that, like Bethsaida, the settlement did not recover from this event and remained unoccupied for an extended time. Amihai Mazar notes that Tiglath-Pileser III conquered the Galilee in 732 BCE and lists that Samaria, Dan, Hazor, Megiddo, and Tizrah, among the major Israelite cities, and Tel Zeror, Tel Qadesh, Tell Qiri, Shiqmona, Dothan, and Shechem, among the smaller towns and villages, all suffered destruction during the Assyrian conquests.[10]

Because of this complete destruction of much of the area, and in particular of Bethsaida, there is no subsequent continuity of culture at these locations. Unlike the kingdoms of Moab, Ammon, or Edom which benefited and prospered from a peaceful surrender of autonomy to the advancing Assyrians, Bethsaida was never incorporated into the Assyrian administration that reorganized the area subsequent to the first phase in Stern's schema.

Likewise we do not have any evidence of Assyrian repopulation which is characteristic of some other areas affected by the first penetration and destruction by the Assyrians. This is unlike what occurred in those areas affected by the second phase of the Assyrian expansion into the southern areas of Palestine. The Iron IIC which follows after the Assyrian conquest is a period of substantial growth for many southern, that is Judean, towns and cities. Presumably this is because of an influx of refugees from the now destroyed northern kingdom of Israel. The same holds true for Moabite and Edomite towns as well.[11] Younker employs the term *pax assyriaca* when referring to this phenomena. He notes that many towns and cities in Judah, for example, Jerusalem, underwent significant growth. He also lists towns in Moab and Edom that likewise show increased development during this time

In the years between 545 and 538 BCE, Palestine and generally the whole of the Middle East came under the dominion of the Achaemenid Persians.[12] The Achaemenid empire at its greatest extent stretched across the whole of the region from North Africa to Southern Russian, including the areas of Asia Minor to the Indus. The whole of Palestine was merely a minor part of the bureaucracy that divvied up the vast empire into twenty-some regional units or satrapies that were then subdivided into secondary districts. The region that included Palestine and Bethsaida was known as formerly under the Assyrians, as "across the river" (the "Transeuphratene") and contained Syria, Phoenicia, and Cyprus along with Palestine. The subdivisions or provinces that are best known to us include sites such as Megiddo, Dor, Samaria, Judea, Ashdod, and Gaza. Each of these locations would have had a resident governor who was responsible to the chief official of the satrapy for all administrative duties and tax collection. This administrative system was in place until the appearance of Alexander in the area and his subsequent conquest of Darius III at Granica in 334 BCE that then led to the rise of the Hellenistic empires as successors of the larger Persian Empire.

The Persian period in Palestine is one of the more obscure periods in the region. The biblical material does not contain much beyond a few somewhat inconsistent bits of information and certainly does not give clear evidence for how the administrative culture of the Persian empire may have affected the daily activities of the Galilee region. Likewise, despite a recent rise in interest in research on the history of the Persian Empire, its domination over the "Transeuphratene," the region "Beyond the River" [Euphrates] designated in the biblical text as *"eber-han-nahar,"* remains quite poorly known. Despite its importance as one of the three principal regions of the Persian Empire in particular, along with the regions of Assyria and Akkad, or in any of the prior empires that governed the area, it is very difficult to even speak of the political structure that the Persians employed.[13] The political structure may have incorporated the inherited territorial subdivisions from preceding adjudicata. In fact, the boundaries of the territory are somewhat fluid and dependent on intraterritorial events that might change the boundaries of semi-autonomous subregions that had their own frontiers—like those of the Phoenician coastal cities.[14] This in some way would explain the uncontested expansion from the coastal cities to the "empty" region of the Galilee.

All of the above would seem to prioritize the importance of the material culture of the region for recovering some fuller picture of the history of the period. Unfortunately, the archaeological record seems to be equally unclear at this point. It is not uncommon to see only the notation concerning "some scant remains from the Persian period" in a dig report, such as that of the Tel Zayit report.[15] Yet, Charles Carter notes that Persian control during this period is marked by both an expansionist vision and a new system of enhanced social control. Cyrus exhibits the cohesive social policy that sought to influence the area through repatriation and religious initiative, while subsequent rulers such as Cambyses and Darius sought to expand and consolidate power through military campaign.[16] However, because of the political upheaval that both precedes and follows this rather long period of stability, sites that contain a clear Persian occupation strata are either reoccupied and disturbed or left unoccupied and subject to surface contamination.

While more recent excavations have mitigated this problem to some extent by providing clearly stratified contexts with accompanying homogeneous assemblages, because the Persian period falls between the First and Second Temple periods, few archaeologists have focused specifically on this time frame. Even among those who do, many find that the later Hellenistic and Roman occupation of many Persian period sites damaged or destroyed the earlier levels of occupation.[17] Ephraim Stern's work represents one of the early attempts to codify and present the Persian period finds and settlement patterns to give a coherent picture of life during these centuries. However, the material remains for the Galilee region are sparse at best. The sites listed by Stern do not directly present any parallels that might help us to understand the extent of occupation that may have been present in the Bethsaida region. At best, they suggest that there was no significant population present in the area immediate to Bethsaida.

As noted above, the transition from Iron II to Persian periods is of particular interest for the present investigation. At Bethsaida, there is very little evidence of occupation from the Persian period and what is in evidence seems to be from the earlier transitional period before distinctive Persian-period traditions are established in pottery, architecture, or weaponry. The chief archaeologist for the Bethsaida Excavations Project, Dr. Rami Arav, has indicated that the sparse evidence for Persian period occupation that has been recovered on the site is based "mostly on stratigraphy and not pottery."[18] This may be confirmation of Charles Carter's observation that at the beginning of the period the material culture from the Persian period may not be recoverable on the basis of pottery since it shows a continuation of Iron II pottery traditions.[19] This means that there are more clearly datable strata above or below what has been labeled as Persian period. Thus, strata bracketed by Iron II and Hellenistic materials are assumed to be Persian period. Therefore, there exists only a very tentative attribution of date to those layers based solely upon relative dating.

It follows that if the meager Persian occupation at Bethsaida was not continuous, then we would not expect to find the later more clearly recognizable forms in the recovered material culture. This would correspond to Bethsaida's having been occupied only during what Carter terms as the Persian I period, which is designated as prior to the shift in imperial policy that begins the fortification of the western frontier against a growing Greek threat.[20] This suggests that we may have discovered only a small temporary and perhaps solely military presence, although it must be said that no clearly distinguished military equipment from the period has been recovered to date.

The fact that the recovered Persian material and associated strata are found "between the gate and the plaza of the Bit Hilani palace"[21] may also confirm this suggestion. The small finds from this area that are likely from the Persian period consist of a cylinder seal and an enigmatic glass token.[22] Baruch Brandl describes the cylinder seal as "an Achaemenian product" on the basis of its art motifs. Because it evidences a great deal of Assyrian and Phoenician influence on those motifs, he further refines its dating to the earlier part of this period. Also, he posits, based upon its quality, that the seal is not locally made and thus may indicate an actual physical Persian presence on the site.[23] This, too, may confirm the "military hypothesis." Or, as Carter notes, "The most common understanding of the seal impressions is that they were used in the collection of taxes in the form of in-kind contributions or that they were used in trade."[24] Carter further states that he would expect seals to be found more widely spread throughout the province if the seals had more of a trade aspect than taxation. Bethsaida might then present evidence for the latter understanding since it is evident that it was by no means an administrative center for collecting imperial taxes from the local populace.

In any event, there is certainly no significant population present at Bethsaida during the Persian period. The possible Persian period presence is limited to a small area of the tell and also probably did not continue throughout the period. It was likely to have been only a brief military presence at the beginning of the transitional time from the end of the Iron II period. It may be that when the Persian administration overspread the region, the mound of Et-Tell/ Bethsaida was made a watchpost. We clearly do not see a vibrant or even viable urban settlement at the site during this time. There is no indication that following the destruction during the eighth century BCE the site remained continually populated in any significant numbers.

In what may be a somewhat ironic statement, Arav notes that "it is not too much but the mound was not totally vacant."[25] The same might be said concerning much of the entire Galilee region. Carter notes that in the province of Yehud, which is an extensive territory containing much of earlier Judah, there were eighty-six settlements in the Persian I period. This expands to 125 during the Persian II period, and he suggests a population of 13,350 at the beginning of the Persian I period growing by 55 percent to 20,650 by the mid to late Persian II period. This figure is strikingly lower than that of the area prior to the Assyrian conquest! In fact, it is estimated that Iron Age Bethsaida alone would have housed a population of nearly 2000 or what would have been 10 percent of the entire province of Yehud.

Carter further notes that during much of the Neo-Babylonian period the city of Jerusalem in the province of Yehud was left in ruins and that Tell en-Nasbeh [Mizpah] functioned as the regional capital until early in the Persian period.[26] Thus, Jerusalem's re-ascendancy followed the application of Cyrus's policies of repatriation and establishment of indigenous religious centers. This pattern, however, does not appear repeated in the Bethsaida context. It would appear that Bethsaida, which was destroyed during the Assyrian campaigns prior to the Neo-Babylonian campaigns of a century later, was not recognized as a regional religious/ethnic center as were Jerusalem and other sites in the wider region.

This would mean that there was no indigenous population in the area during most of the Persian period and, accordingly, no continuation of cultural legacy from the prior Iron Age society. This observation has an immediate bearing on some reconstructions of the social matrix present in the first century CE.

PERSIAN TO HELLENISTIC PERIOD TRANSITION

In the Hellenistic period, most of the mountainous part of Galilee was settled with a few large sites and small villages, some of which were occupied for only part of the year. This population probably comprised mainly peasants from the Phoenician mountains (the area between the Phoenician coast and the Ituraean Baqa' Valley), alongside the remnants of the inhabitants from earlier periods. The main characteristics of the material culture of this population are the Galilean Course Ware (GCW) vessels and the local cult objects.[27] As we have stated above, Bethsaida is outside of the region of Iron Age Galilee. In addition, Bethsaida does not appear to have "remnants" of inhabitants from the earlier period. Instead, we witness at Bethsaida a repopulation from the coast. This presumably occurred from the coastal region of Tyre/Ptolemais.[28] As Mordechai Aviam notes, it was at the start of the Hellenistic period that "[o]n the edges of the Galilee, four large metropolises emerged: Tyre in the north, Akko-Ptolemais in the southwest, Bet Shean-Scythopolis in the southeast and Sussita-Hippos in the east."[29] These are clearly Hellenistic pagan[30] sites that continue into the first century, two on the Phoenician coast and two in what later becomes the Decapolis.

Bethsaida's reoccupation in some ways parallels that described for many of the Decapolis cities, as exemplified by Susita, which were founded or refounded shortly following Alexander the Great's death. Arthur Segal notes that "pottery from [Sussita] found beneath a Hellenistic compound indicates that the site was first inhabited by the Ptolemies in the third century BCE. Whether it was a semi-urban settlement or simply an outpost fortress is still uncertain, although the latter seems more likely."[31] This closely resembles what we see at Bethsaida. As we shall see in chapter 4, the material culture of Bethsaida suddenly has a resurgence during the same Ptolemaic expansion in the third century BCE. The ceramic corpus and associated small finds dramatically increase from the almost negligible Persian finds, and the stylistic patterns in the ceramic assemblage are oriented now toward the Phoenician coast rather than the north and east as it was during the Iron Age. This resurgence also includes a substantial architectural program as well. Numerous Hellenistic courtyard houses appear, along with several other more public structures.[32]

However, the history of Bethsaida diverges from that reported by Segal for Sussita following the refounding. Sussita was conquered by Alexander Janneus in 83–80 BCE, much later it seems than Bethsaida's incorporation into the Hasmonean sphere of influence, and it never really became incorporated as a Jewish city. The city was given to the Province of Syria when the Romans reorganized the area following their entrance to and political control of the region in 63 BCE. Even though it is again transferred to Herod the Great in 37 BCE when he assumes governmental responsibility for his Roman patrons as a client king, it is immediately transferred back to Syria in 4 BCE following his death at the behest of the citizens. Thus, Segal speaks of a "Jewish minority" at Sussita, but Sussita does not have the significant transformation of the site's material culture from pagan to Jewish as we recognize at Bethsaida.[33]

As we shall see in chapter 4, thus, the material culture of Bethsaida suddenly has a resurgence in the Hellenistic period. The ceramic corpus and associated small finds dramatically increase from the almost negligible Persian finds, and its stylistic patterns are oriented now toward the Phoenician coast rather than the north and east as it was during the Iron Age. This resurgence also includes a substantial architectural program as well. Numerous Hellenistic courtyard houses appear, along with several other more public structures.[34]

THE HASMONEAN REVOLUTION: LATE HELLENISTIC TO EARLY ROMAN TRANSITION

We know from literary sources that the Hasmonean rulers were active in acquiring influence and territory in the Galilee, in Samaria and along the Phoenician coast. 1 Maccabees 11:67 describes Jonathan's early foray in the region nearby Et-Tell/Bethsaida mentioning his encampment near the waters of Gennesaret, which is commonly assumed to be in the area of Migdal but could possibly be more correctly located closer to the plain near Bethsaida.[35] 1 Maccabees and Josephus both detail much of the Hasmonean activity and its impact on the region.[36] Archaeological evidence now shows that there were ethnic and religious changes in Galilee at the end of the second century BCE.

> The newest evidence that supports the conquest and the resettlement of Jews in Galilee is a numismatic survey of Hasmonean coins. This survey identified many of these coins in areas that are known in later periods to be Jewish according to remains of synagogues. In contrast, there is almost a total lack of these coins in areas known to be inhabited by gentiles, like Akko.[37]

This change can be seen in the significant increase in the number of settlements in the area into what may be termed marginal agricultural areas. Uzi Leibner, in his unpublished dissertation, notes that: "The number of settlements in comparison to the Hellenistic period doubled and so did the size of the settled area beginning during the first century BCE and continuing into the first century CE."[38] He adds that on the basis of his "high resolution survey," which depends on the collection of large samples of pottery that with careful analysis allows categorizing the survey pottery into short duration sub-periods, he is able to make a precise determination about the number of settled sites, which peaks during this time frame. While the population continues to increase in most areas in the subsequent early Roman and Byzantine periods, according to Leibner, the range of settlement remains fairly constant.

Thus, what is generally seen in this survey of the Eastern half of the Galilee is that there is a dramatic change in both the material corpus and the numbers of inhabitants. Andrea Berlin also notes this change during the Hasmonean expansion in the latter half of the second century BCE. She remarks that "many new Jewish settlements appeared, laid out as both agricultural villages and strategic outposts,"[39] the number of which increased nearly threefold in the Galilee and Hula Valley.

However, in areas previously containing non-Jewish population she points out that the later Hasmonean destruction and acquisition created a clear change in material culture. At Gamla, for example, after Janneus exercised control by appointing the mayor, the ceramic corpus changes to a plethora of undecorated, local pottery. Berlin argues that this transition from the Eastern Sigillata A (ESA) and other wares that were common from the Phoenician coast is not the result of economic downturn, but conscious choice. She bases this observation in part on the fact that the excavations at Gamla discovered several large commercial oil presses and thousands of coins, indicating a profitable economic situation.[40]

This dramatic shift in material culture appears in the Bethsaida record as well. However, the level of prosperity does not appear to equal the level of economic prosperity that Berlin finds at Gamla. As the coin evidence examined in the next chapter may indicate, Bethsaida seems to decline from the level of prosperity experienced prior to the transition from Seleucid to Jewish control. Nonetheless, the complete disappearance of the other wares cannot simply be

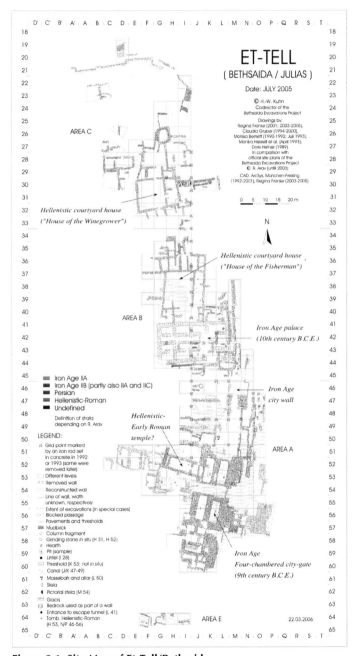

Figure 3.1. Site Map of Et-Tell/Bethsaida
Source: Professor emeritus Dr. Heinz-Wolfgang Kuhn, Ludwig-Maximilians-Universität München

Figure 3.2. Balloon Photo of Tell
Source: Paul Bauman, Principal Geophysicist, WorleyParsons Komex

explained on the basis of economic downturn. The constellation of other Jewish ethnic markers found at Bethsaida, in conjunction with the ceramic transition, may indeed support her argument for the conscious nonappropriation of ESA and other wares.

We will explore this topic further in the next chapter.

NOTES

1. Israel Finkelstein notes that in his view this process of Israelite settlement began no earlier than the twelfth century BCE and continued into the early tenth century BCE progressing southward in the central hill country in the north to finally Judah in the south as indicated by the relocation of the cultic center from Shiloh to Judah. Israel Finkelstein, *The Archaeology of the Israelite Settlement* (Jerusalem: Israel Exploration Society, 1988), 353–55. While allowing for the existence of a Davidic monarchy, Finkelstein's minimalist view of the existence of the united monarchy remains less grand than traditional images. Israel Finkelstein and Neil Asher Silberman,

David and Solomon in Search of the Bible's Sacred Kings and the Roots of the Western Tradition (New York: Free Press, 2006), 281.

2. Amihai Mazar, *Archaeology of the Land of the Bible: 10,000–586 B.C.E.*, Anchor Bible Reference Library (New York: Doubleday, 1990), 397–98.

3. This is Amihai Mazar's periodization of the Iron Age period in the Levant. Mazar, *Archaeology of the Land of the Bible: 10,000–586 B.C.E.*, 30.

4. The use of Iron III seems somewhat muddled. Schoville refers to it as circa 600–332 B.C. but in the text states "Iron Age III, or the Persian period, was ushered in . . . 539 B.C." Keith N. Schoville, *Biblical Archaeology in Focus* (Grand Rapids, MI: Baker Book House, 1978), 56. In general, however, the designation seems to be applied to the Neo-Babylonian period of Israelite history, 598/7–539 BCE.

5. See Pierre Briant, *From Cyrus to Alexander: A History of the Persian Empire* (Winona Lake, IN: Eisenbrauns, 2002).

6. Charles E. Carter, "Syria-Palestine in the Persian Period," in *Near Eastern Archaeology: A Reader*, ed. Suzanne Richard (Winona Lake, IN: Eisenbrauns, 2003), 399.

7. Randall W. Younker, "The Iron Age in the Southern Levant," in *Near Eastern Archaeology: A Reader*, ed. Suzanne Richard (Winona Lake, IN: Eisenbrauns, 2003), 377–79.

8. See figure 3.1, Site Map of Et-Tell/Bethsaida, page 66.

9. Ephraim Stern, *Archaeology of the Land of the Bible: The Assyrian, Babylonian, and Persian Periods, 732–332 BCE*, Anchor Bible Reference Library (New York: Doubleday, 2001), 3.

10. Mazar, *Archaeology of the Land of the Bible: 10,000–586 B.C.E.*, 540.

11. Younker, "The Iron Age in the Southern Levant," 379.

12. Briant discusses this in some detail. Briant, *From Cyrus to Alexander: A History of the Persian Empire*, 44–49. See also Ephraim Stern, *Archaeology of the Land of the Bible: The Assyrian, Babylonian, and Persian Periods, 732–332 BCE*, 353f.

13. Two recent studies may alleviate this obscurity and difficulty: Lisbeth S. Fried, *The Priest and the Great King Temple-Palace Relations in the Persian Empire* (Winona Lake, IN: Eisenbrauns, 2004), and Kenneth G. Hoglund, *Achaemenid Imperial Administration in Syria-Palestine and the Missions of Ezra and Nehemiah* (Atlanta, GA: Scholars Press, 1992).

14. Josette Elayi and Jean Sapin, *Beyond the River: New Perspectives on Transeuphratene*, Journal for the Study of the Old Testament (Sheffield, UK: Sheffield Academic Press, 1998), 17.

15. Ron E. Tappy et al., "An Abecedary of the Mid-Tenth Century B.C.E.," *Bulletin of the American Schools of Oriental Research* 344 (November 2006): 7.

16. Carter, "Syria-Palestine in the Persian Period," 402.

17. Elayi and Sapin, *Beyond the River: New Perspectives on Transeuphratene*, 19.

18. Rami Arav, personal email (2007). However, Sandra Fortner in her unpublished dissertation does record a very few disinctive Persian pottery types. See Sandra Ann Fortner, "Die Keramik und Kleinfunde von Bethsaida Am See Genezareth, Israel," unpublished dissertation (University of Munich, 2005).

19. Carter, "Syria-Palestine in the Persian Period," 399.

20. Carter, "Syria-Palestine in the Persian Period," 399–400. .

21. Arav, personal email.

22. While working in this general area during the 2000 season, the author did recover the only recognizable pieces of Iron Age IIc pottery he has personally seen on the site. These consisted of several rim fragments from cooking pots.

23. Baruch Brandl, "Two First-Millennium Cylinder Seals from Bethsaida (Et-Tell)," in *Bethsaida: A City by the North Shore of the Sea of Galilee* (Kirksville, MO: Truman State University Press, 1999), 235–36. Rami Arav, in a personal email, indicates that "years ago Brandl presented a piece of a bronze decoration of a chair which is typical to the Persian period. The bronze was found at the sea of Galilee in the vicinity of Bethsaida and he thought that it may have originated there." Again, it would seem to indicate some kind of "regional presence" but not a specifically significant settled occupation at Bethsaida.

24. Carter, "Syria-Palestine in the Persian Period," 410.

25. Arav, personal email.

26. Carter, "Syria-Palestine in the Persian Period," 406.

27. Aviam, *Jews, Pagans, and Christians in the Galilee: 25 Years of Archaeological Excavations and Surveys: Hellenistic to Byzantine Periods*, 315.

28. This supposition is supported from the ceramic and coin evidence at Bethsaida, see Chapter 4. Also the position finds support in the work of Andrea Berlin on Phoenician semi-fine ware distribution and Hellenistic settlement patterns. See Andrea M. Berlin, "From Monarchy to Markets: The Phoenicians in Hellenistic Palestine," *Bulletin of the American Schools of Oriental Research* 306 (May 1997): 75–88.

29. Aviam, *Jews, Pagans, and Christians in the Galilee: 25 Years of Archaeological Excavations and Surveys: Hellenistic to Byzantine Periods*, 315.

30. One is reminded that we are employing Chancey's definition of "pagan" and that pagan site in this sense indicates only a non-Jewish polytheistic population center.

31. Arthur Segal, "The Spade Hits Sussita," *The Biblical Archaeology Review* 32 (May/June 2006): 43. Segal indicates that this is a new inhabitation and not one that displaces or assimilates any prior populace.

32. See figure 3.1, Site Map of Et-Tell/Bethsaida, page 66, and figure E1.1 Map of Area A Showing Hellenistic/Roman Features, page 151.

33. Segal, "The Spade Hits Sussita," 45.

34. See figure 4.15, Map of Area B, page 101, in addition to the maps mentioned previously.

35. "Meanwhile, Jonathan and his army pitched their camp near the waters of Gennesaret, and at daybreak they went to the plain of Hazor." 1 Maccabees 11:67. Jonathan Goldstein in his commentary on the events of this campaign notes that there is a possibility that the family of one of Jonathan's steadfast commanders traced its lineage to the "house of Absalom." This would make an interesting connection to Bethsaida as that, if the researchers' present conjecture is correct, Et-Tell was the likely home of Absalom's maternal family. See Goldstein, *I Maccabees: A New Translation, with Introduction and Commentary*, 441–43, particularly the note on verses 68–70, 443.

36. See, for example, much of 1 Maccabees 11 and Josephus *Antiquites* xiii 9:1f.

37. Mordechai Aviam, "First Century Jewish Galilee," in *Religion and Society in Roman Palestine: Old Questions, New Approaches*, ed. Douglas R. Edwards (New York: Routledge, 2004), 14–15.

38. Uzi Leibner, "History of Settlement in the Eastern Galilee During the Hellenistic, Roman and Byzantine Periods in Light of an Archaeological Survey," PhD dissertation (Ramet-Gan, Israel: Bar-Ilan University, 2004). Dr. Leibner graciously shared his abstract and conclusions with the author. He surveyed forty-six sites in the Eastern Galilee region, collecting over two hundred diagnostic potsherds from each site for the periods of his investigation.

39. Andrea M. Berlin, "The Hellenistic Period," in *Near Eastern Archaeology: A Reader*, ed. Suzanne Richard (Winona Lake, IN: Eisenbrauns, 2003), 423–24.

40. Berlin, "The Hellenistic Period," 428. See also Danny Syon and Zvi Yavor, "Gamla Old and New," *Qadmoniot* 34, no. 1 (2001).

4

SUPPORTING EVIDENCE FOR FIRST CENTURY CE BETHSAIDA

The nature of the question of evidence for a first century Bethsaida incorporates a lot of the surrounding presumptions of what the first century looked like in the Galilee region. To quote Mark A. Chancey on the matter: "Indeed one wonders if some scholars have started with the view that Galilee's population was mixed and then searched for reasons to explain why it was so."[1] Chancey also makes the point that "the presence of Hellenism at a site does not necessarily indicate the presence of pagans, and the presence of pagans does not necessarily imply the presence of Hellenism."[2] That observation contravenes many of the earlier studies, as reflected in the language that F. E. Peters employs, namely that "since the days of the Greek colonization in the wake of Alexander [the residents of Galilee] lived in an atmosphere dominated by Hellenism and the Hellenized Syrians who ruled the cities."[3] Peters' comments are echoed or presaged in many studies that may be organized into two basic categories, those assuming a bucolic Galilee or those emphasizing an urbanized Galilee. The varying views include a kind of "ghettoized" division between urban Hellenism and rural Judaism, one that expects "Athens-on-the-Kinneret" but with Talmudic villages in the vicinity, that is, villages with characteristics more typical of post–first century CE Judaism.[4]

These perspectives, albeit somewhat caricatured, represent the influence of religious and literary preconceptions of what life must have been like in the first century CE. I do not wish to take on this larger question, but simply to state that neither pole reflects what we uncover at Bethsaida during the time period in question. Although Bethsaida represents only one site and not the whole region, other recent surveys seem to concur with the findings at Bethsaida.[5]

This chapter proposes to simply put out the evidence we have that there was an occupation of Et-Tell/Bethsaida throughout the Hellenistic period, beginning during the time of the Ptolemaic/Seleucid struggle for control of the region and ending sometime before the Byzantine empire's ascendancy.

As stated above in chapter 3, Arthur Segal, excavating at Sussita, also traces its origins to this same period. His description of the foundations of this Decapolis city closely resembles that of Bethsaida. In that regard, I propose to give a "brief history of time" at Et-Tell, indicating a plausible reason for its reoccupation after destruction in the Iron Age II, and showing that it was inhabited during the first century CE, leaving aside a consideration of its eventual demise sometime before the Byzantine period.[6] This history begins with the same story as at Sussita but varies considerably in its later development.[7]

I wish to illustrate this with reference to key material indicators that we have found at Bethsaida: coins, stamped amphora handles, glassware, ceramics, stoneware, and architectural remains. All of these indicators taken singularly are not as compelling as seeing them as an interrelated whole, of course.

Before turning to the material finds, let me briefly state my proposed time line for the occupation of Et-Tell during the Hellenistic period.

TIMELINE TO THE FIRST CENTURY CE

Et-Tell was destroyed sometime during the Iron Age II, ostensibly during the Assyrian conquest of the region in the late eighth century.[8] There is clear evidence of massive destruction at the huge Iron Age city-gate as well as little evidence of occupation for nearly five centuries following that catastrophic event. There have been only very fragmentary finds from the Iron Age III and Persian periods and no evidence of construction during these times.

What we see instead is a sudden period of construction and reoccupation beginning during the Hellenistic period in the third century BCE. On the basis of the coin evidence this may have occurred during the reign of Ptolemy II, perhaps prior to the First Syrian War (274–271 BCE), as a significant number of Ptolemy II coins have been found at Bethsaida.[9] However, Donald Ariel suggests a later date based upon the stamped handles and the fact that coins may remain in circulation well beyond their mint dates.[10] Jodi Magness, at the recent conference at Yale on "The Ancient Galilee in Interaction: Religion, Ethnicity and Identity," issued the same caution when considering coinage for dating occupations and constructions.[11] Perhaps one could concede that reoccupation may have occurred later in the third century BCE but one must admit that there certainly was a Ptolemaic presence in the area since coins of Ptolemy III are also present. However, control seems to pass to the Seleucids in the time of Antiochus III following the fourth Syrian War (217 BCE), perhaps as late as 200 BCE. We find no Ptolemaic coins after the reign of Ptolemy III, that is, none later than 222 BCE.[12] There is no evidence of destruction at the site during this transition period, merely a change in coinage that would indicate a change of governmental orientation. Seleucid control appears to be maintained until John Hyrcanus I's expansion into the Golan area in the late second century BCE. Again, control seems to be "peaceably" transferred. There is no evidence of destruction, although there are significant changes in the total material culture and not just in the coinage.[13] The ceramic finds seem to indicate an altered pattern of exchange. This change at the site seems to affirm Andrea Berlin's observation that the expansion of the Hasmonean Kingdom resulted in the Mediterranean oriented culture of the earlier Hellenistic period being replaced by "material simplification and economic isolation."[14] Likewise we see evidence in the coin sequence

Table 4.1.   Coin Frequency at Bethsaida by Dynasty

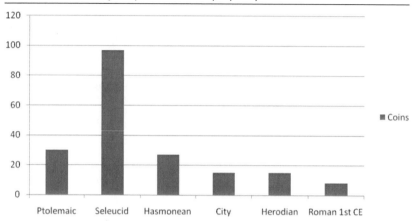

of a transition to Herodian control as part of Herod's assuming the throne. Herodian coins appear in the coinage at Et-Tell/Bethsaida, continuing an unbroken sequence of Jewish coinage following the Hasmonean period.

Thus, Bethsaida may have been established during a relatively peaceful time of expansion from the more settled Phoenician coast. There is some possibility that the earliest settlers were military veterans. This comes in part from the presence of Rhodian wine amphoras, which have been suggested by some as a marker for military presence.[15] Donald Ariel holds that "there may be some cogency in suggesting that, in table 4.1. Coin Sequence of Bethsaida by Ruler,[16] the last third of the third century BCE, there was a military outpost at Bethsaida."[17] He notes that the earliest settlement at Gamla has now also been explained on that basis by Syon and Yavor.[18] The fact that Bethsaida is located at the conjunction of two of the passes in the road system of the Golan that were among the six western entrances to the region creates a viable context for this possibility. Ariel notes that this notion of a military outpost origin for Bethsaida would explain its sudden appearance. However, there are no obvious signs of Bethsaida having been a military outpost—in the form of towers, gates, and fortifications or Hellenistic military artifacts— other than this amphora connection.[19] Perhaps it may be better to

Table 4.2.   Distribution of Bethsaida Coins by Ruler

Ruler	Date of Reign	Number of Coins Excavated
Ptolemy II	284–246 BCE	17
Ptolemy III	246–222 BCE	14
Antiochus III	223–187 BCE	31
Antiochus IV	175–164 BCE	6
Antiochus V	164–162 BCE	4
Demetrius I	161–150 BCE	5
Demetrius II (first reign)	145–138 BCE	11
Antiochus VII	138–129 BCE	5
Demetrius II (second reign)	129–126 BCE	11
John Hyrcanus I	134–104 BCE	5
Aristobulus I	104–103 BCE	1
Alexander Jannaeus	103–76 BCE	9
Aristobulus II	66–63 BCE	4
Hyrcanus II	63–40 BCE	1
Herod	37–4 BCE	3
Herod Archelaus	4 BCE–6 CE	1
Herod Antipas	4 BCE–40 CE	1
Philip	4 BCE–34 CE	4
Agrippa I	37–44 CE	1
Agrippa II	55–95 CE	3

suggest that veterans might have settled the site rather than active military personnel. In any event, the amphoras and coin evidence both seem to indicate a renewed presence at Bethsaida beginning in the mid to latter third century BCE.

COINS

Over two hundred coins have been recovered at Bethsaida from the relevant Hellenistic, Hasmonean, Herodian, and early Roman periods. While there are a few that predate the reconstructed occupational history that I propose,[20] the earlier coins, particularly because they tend to be large denomination silver coins, may have been still in circulation during the time of earliest reoccupation (i.e., circulated for more than one hundred years). One may argue to some extent about the precise terminus a quo for this reoccupation, but the bulk of the evidence suggests that it did begin during the reign of Ptolemy II (309–246 BCE).

The coin data is cited from Arieh Kindler's work on the coins of Bethsaida.[21] Working from not only his published reports but his individual coin reports as well, and incorporating some suggested revisions by Donald Ariel and myself, I have developed the distribution patterns that are indicated in the coin distribution charts, tables 4.1 and 4.3.[22]

Ilan Shachar graciously allowed me to read his unpublished MA thesis[23] in which he examines the Bethsaida coins in light of his contention that one may use the presence of Jannaeus type 7 coins to establish continuous inhabitation during the late second century BCE on into the first century BCE. More precisely, he suggests that the absence of Jannaeus type 7 coins is indicative of a site that was conquered and destroyed by Jannaeus.

Under this theory, later Herodian or Roman imperial coinage would indicate a resettlement but not a continuous occupation. While this hypothesis sounds feasible to some extent, the fact that in the Bethsaida collection there are nine Hasmonean coins and more than forty Seleucid coins that are relatively unidentifiable, coupled with the fact that type 7 coins are "degenerative, crude

Table 4.3. Coin Distribution by Century

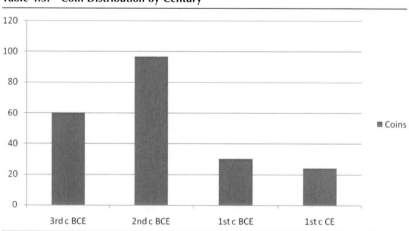

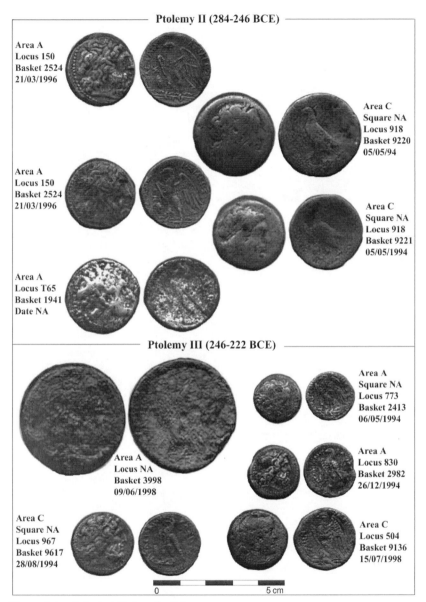

Figure 4.1. Selected Ptolemaic Coins
Source: Carl E. Savage

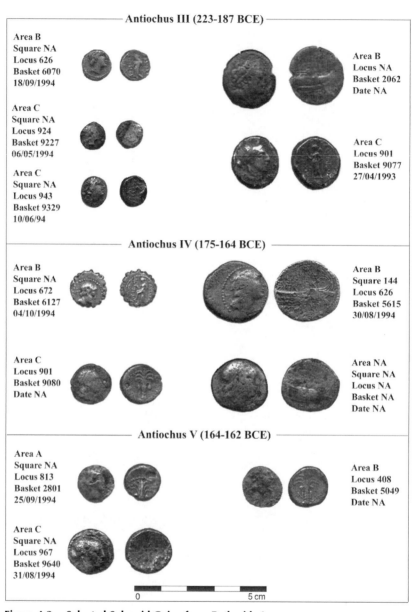

Figure 4.2.   Selected Seleucid Coins from Bethsaida I
Source: Carl E. Savage

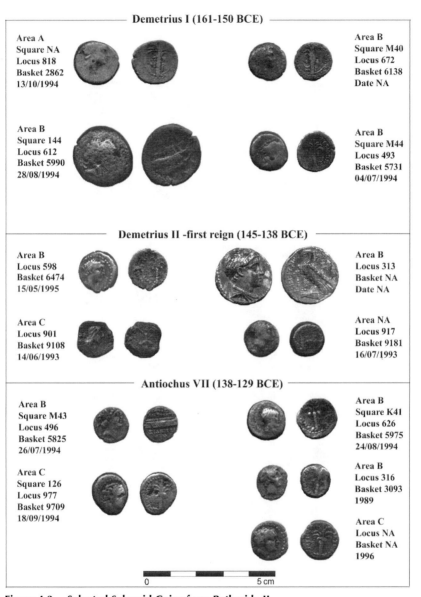

Figure 4.3. Selected Seleucid Coins from Bethsaida II
Source: Carl E. Savage

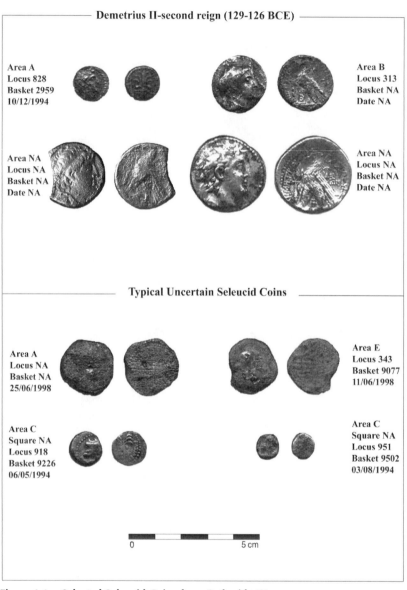

Figure 4.4. Selected Seleucid Coins from Bethsaida III
Source: Carl E. Savage

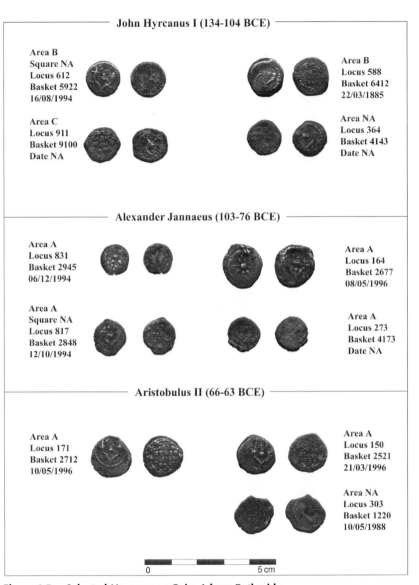

Figure 4.5. Selected Hasmonean Coins I from Bethsaida
Source: Carl E. Savage

Selected Hasmonean Coins II

Typical Uncertain Hasmonean Coins

Area A
Locus 173
Basket 2713
10/05/1996

Area A
Locus 150
Basket 2515
20/03/1996

Area B
Locus 314
Basket NA
Date NA

Area NA
Locus 301
Basket 1208
13/03/1988

Area A
Locus 273
Basket 4173
Date NA

Sected Herodian Coins I

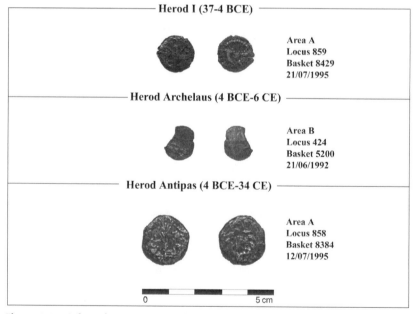

Herod I (37-4 BCE)

Area A
Locus 859
Basket 8429
21/07/1995

Herod Archelaus (4 BCE-6 CE)

Area B
Locus 424
Basket 5200
21/06/1992

Herod Antipas (4 BCE-34 CE)

Area A
Locus 858
Basket 8384
12/07/1995

0   5 cm

Figure 4.6.   Selected Hasmonean Coins II and Selected Herodian Coins I
Source: Carl E. Savage

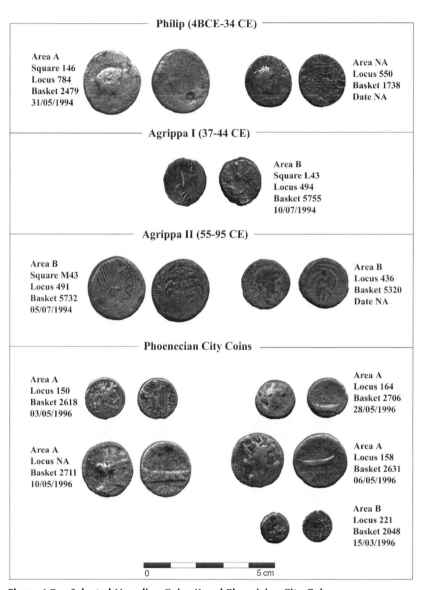

Figure 4.7. Selected Herodian Coins II and Phoenician City Coins
Source: Carl E. Savage

copies or imitations of Type 5" and negligently made,[24] allows the possibility that some type 7 Jannaeus coins are present but remain unrecognized among those coins described as "uncertain." Shachar states that he sees a numismatic gap of forty years indicative of destruction similar to what he notes for Pella. However, while this may be theoretically possible, there is no destruction layer at Bethsaida, and Shachar may not take sufficiently into account the city coins whose dates would also occupy some of the gap that he sees in the numismatic record of Bethsaida. In any event, even according to Shachar's theory, Bethsaida would have been quickly resettled by the Herodians in the late first century BCE as indicated by the sequence of Herodian coins. So whereas the Bethsaida evidence does not seem to fit with his assessment of the occupation record based upon his theory in regard to Jannaeus type 7 coins, his work fits with the view that Bethsaida was occupied during the first century CE.[25]

RHODIAN STAMPED HANDLES

Fourteen stamped handles have been recovered in the Bethsaida excavations through the 2004 season. All of these are of the Rhodian type, which is the most common type found in the larger region. Large numbers of unstamped imported amphora handles[26] have also been found but they do not contribute much to the chronological understanding of Bethsaida in the Hellenistic period. The stamped handles, however, do provide a second source of evidence for our understanding of the "founding" of Bethsaida during the third century BCE. As seen above, Bethsaida yields many more coins than stamped handles but, as noted, coins generally remain in circulation much longer than amphoras and so the stamped handles may provide a more precise means for dating the occupation of Hellenistic Bethsaida. According to Donald Ariel, the stamped handles indicate that Bethsaida may have been established beginning in the last third of the third century BCE. He notes that ten out of the fourteen handles derive from that period "which was not one of particularly high production in Rhodes, or of high importa-

Figure 4.8. Photographs of Rhodian Amphora Stamped Handles I
Source: Christine Dalenta, Bethsaida Staff Photographer

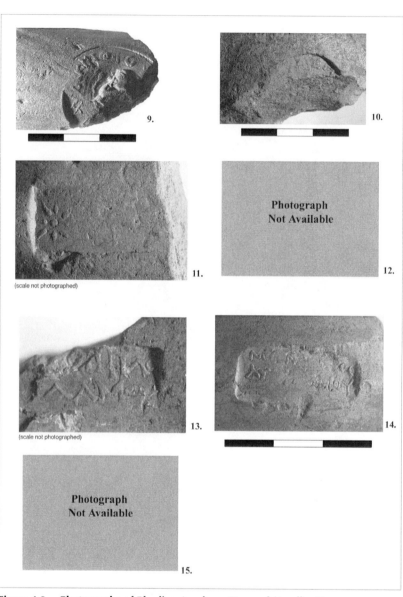

Figure 4.9. Photographs of Rhodian Amphora Stamped Handles II
Source: Christine Dalenta, Bethsaida Staff Photographer

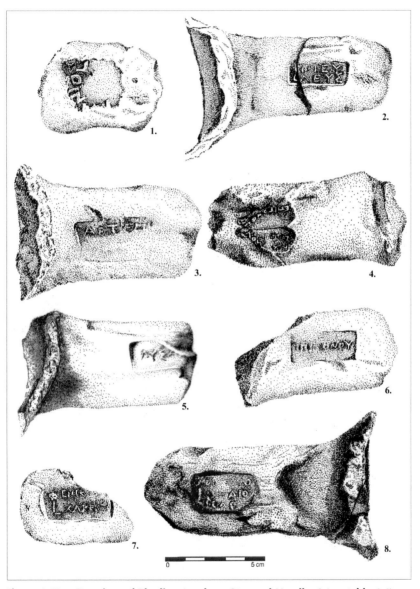

Figure 4.10. Drawings of Rhodian Amphora Stamped Handles I (see table 4.4)
Source: Eric Stegmaier, John and Carol Merrill Qumran Project Staff Artist

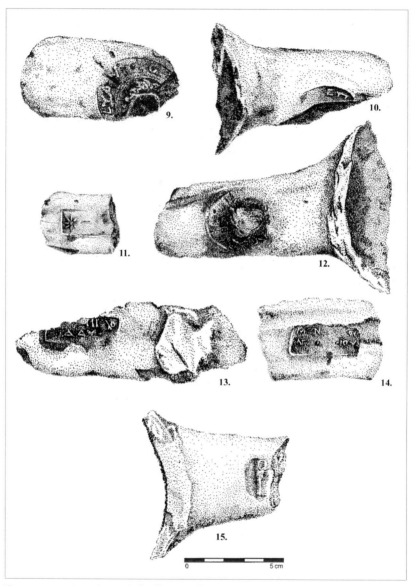

Figure 4.11. Drawings of Rhodian Amphora Stamped Handles II (see table 4.4)
Source: Eric Stegmaier, John and Carol Merrill Qumran Project Staff Artist

Table 4.4. Rhodian Amphora Stamped Handles

	Description	Area: Locus: Basket:	Special Features	Analysis and Parallels
1.	Handle shard	A 807 2749	Rounded irregular/ entire stamp impression visible	Πανσανίας; Πανσανίας 1st, (c. 234–c. 220 BCE) or Πανσανίας 2nd, (c. 209–c. 199 BCE)
2.	Two handle shards	A 150 2531	Entire stamp impression visible (cracked)	c. 234–c. 220 BCE Finkielsztejn 2001a:105; Jöhrens 1999:24, No. 36
3.	Handle shard/some body connection	A 818 2887	Entire stamp impression visible	Rectangular stamp 'Artemi c. 234–c. 220 BCE Conovici and Irimia 1991:166, No. 315; Jöhrens 1999:39, No. 90; Schuchhardt 1895:452, No. 943= Börker 1998:45, No. 431
4.	Handle shard	A 150 2513	Heart shaped stamp impression/ entirely visible	Ἐπίγονος 1st was the only fabricant employing this unusual shape of stamp. c. 216–c. 205 BCE
5.	Handle shard/ some body connection	A 1708 17679	Partial stamp impression visible	Πανσανίας c. 234–220 or 209–199 BCE
6.	Handle shard	B 671 6142	Entire stamp impression visible	Ἐπίγονος 1st Finkielsztejn 2000:143, CRh7, c. 216–c. 205 BCE.
7.	Handle shard	B NA 3003	Nearly entire stamp impression visible	Helios head from the workshop of Θεύδωρος with eponymn Χάρευj c. 219–c. 210

(continued)

Table 4.4. Rhodian Amphora Stamped Handles (*continued*)

	Description	Area: Locus: Basket:	Special Features	Analysis and Parallels
8.	Handle shard/ some body connection	B 221 2034	Entire stamp impression visible	Mšntwr c. 234–c. 210 BCE, Jöhrens 1999:47, Nos. 114–116; Radulescu, Barbulescu and Buzoianu 1987:72, Nos. 149–150
9.	Handle shard	B 252 6516	Partial round stamp impression visible	by handle style "well into the 2nd century BCE"
10.	Handle shard/ some body connection	B 411 5104	Partial rounded stamp impression visible	Stamp had eponym but only δαφ visible based on style late 3rd century BCE
11.	Handle shard	C 402 2043	Partial stamp impression visible	8 pointed star...likely 'Ariste...daj 2nd c. 198–c. 169/167 BCE Jöhrens 1999: 67, No. 175
12.	Handle shard/ some body connection	C 953 9377	Nearly entire rounded stamp impression visible	The circular stamp contains the name Αριστοκλῆς 2nd a prolific fabricant active c. 171–c. 140 BCE Finkielsztejn 2000:147, CRh 25).
13.	Handle shard	C Sq. E 31/32 1064	Partial stamp impression visible	Ἀγορανας or Μαρσύας, eponym Φιλόδαμοj 2nd officiated c. 183 BCE
14.	Handle shard	C 915 9149	Entire stamp impression visible	Μένων, c. 215–c. 204 BCE Finkielsztejn 2000:143, CRh 6
15.	Handle shard	NA 364 3027	Partial stamp impression visible	Caduceus head

tion into the southern Levant."[27] He suggests that the Ptolemy II (281–246 BCE) coins should be connected to the stamped handles rather than be looked at as an indicator of earlier occupation. That is, the Ptolemy II coins were still in current use during the period of use of the shorter-lived amphoras.[28] Ariel further suggests that since the majority of stamped handles fall within the period before 205 BCE, this might be indicative of a brief occupation in preparation for the Fourth Syrian War (219–216 BCE). The suggestion of a short-lived occupation at this time is based in part on his connection of Rhodian amphorae to a military presence.[29] However, he notes that two of the handles date to the later, peak production period of Rhodian amphoras, 190–160 BCE. Furthermore, the latest clearly datable handle could be as late as 140 BCE and other less well classified handles may even date beyond that to 108 BCE.[30] Here our numismatic evidence supplements the picture and indicates, contra Ariel's contention of a disrupted occupation, a Ptolemaic/Seleucid continuation of occupation until well after the Fourth Syrian War.

So although the stamped handles, which are shown in figures 4.8 through 4.11 and table 4.4,[31] do not add to our first century CE evidence directly, they do help to establish a timeline of occupation that incorporates Bethsaida as a viable population center into the first century BCE. The sequence of handles fails during the Hasmonean period, but this is not surprising in light of other evidence indicating that the importation of goods from the coast and the Mediterranean world declined as the site became oriented more toward the Jewish Galilee. The coin sequence continues throughout the first century BCE and into the first century CE unabated.

GLASS

The glass map,[32] which is based upon the work of Dr. Andrea Rottloff, serves mainly to indicate a continuation of occupation from the Hellenistic period into the early Roman. The stars and ovals are the areas in which Dr. Rottloff has identified characteristic Hellenistic and Roman glassware.

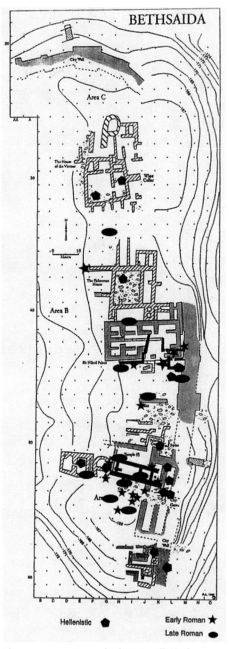

Figure 4.12.   Map of Glass Small Finds
Source: Carl E. Savage, adapted from map of Dr. Andrea
Rottloff

She notes in her initial report on the glass material finds from Bethsaida that there are clear indicative pieces from the Claudian (27 BCE–68 CE) and Flavian (69–96 CE) periods of the Roman Empire as well as a goodly number from the Hellenistic period. She observes that the "most common Hellenistic vessels at Bethsaida are conical or hemispherical molded bowls with incised horizontal lines on the interior surface. . . . They appear from the second century BCE onwards in the whole eastern Mediterranean region."[33] Other common first century BCE types include beakers and bowls characteristic of the period and well attested in other contexts. Rottloff suggests that some of the common household glassware may possibly have been made at Capernaum where Loffreda found a number

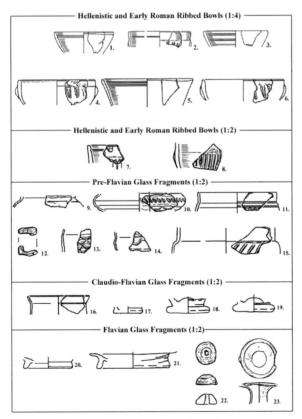

Figure 4.13. Drawings of Glass Small Finds (see table 4.5)
Source: Dr. Andrea Rottloff

Table 4.5. Small Glass Finds

Number	Description	Period	Parallels
1.	Conical molded bowl with incised horizontal lines	2nd century BCE -onward	Avigad 1983, fig 217; Ariel 1990, fig. 27
2.	"Strong-ribbed" bowl	Late Hellenistic–early Roman	Jerusalem, Merion, Tel Anafa
3.	Conical molded bowl with incised horizontal lines	2nd century BCE-onward	Avigad 1983, fig 217; Ariel 1990, fig. 27 (Jerusalem)
4.	"Strong-ribbed" bowl	Late Hellenistic–early Roman	Jerusalem, Meyers et al. 1981 (Meiron) Davidson Weinberg 1970 and 1973 (Tel Anafa)
5.	Conical molded bowl with incised horizontal lines	2nd century BCE -onward	Avigad 1983, fig 217; Ariel 1990, fig. 27
6.	"Strong-ribbed" bowl	Late Hellenistic–early Roman	Jerusalem, Merion, Tel Anafa
7.	"Short ribbed" bowl	Late Hellenistic–early Roman	Jerusalem, Merion, Tel Anafa; Isings form 3c
8.	"Short ribbed" bowl	Late Hellenistic–early Roman	Jerusalem, Merion, Tel Anafa; Isings form 3c
9.	Peacock-blue globular beaker	Pre-69 CE	
10.	Blue-green mold blown cantharos?	Pre-69 CE	
11.	Blue-green mold blown ribbed bowl or beaker	Pre-69 CE	
12.	Brown skyphos handle	Pre-69 CE	
13.	Blue-green mold blown vessel	Pre-69 CE	
14.	Blue-green mold blown vessel	Pre-69 CE	
15.	Blue-green mold blown ribbed bowl or beaker	Pre-69 CE	
16.	Rim of beaker with massive base	27 BCE–96 CE	Isings form 34
17.	Dark blue base	Pre-69 CE	
18.	Beaker with massive base	27 BCE–96 CE	Isings form 34
19.	Beaker with massive base	27 BCE–96 CE	Isings form 34
20.	Bowl base	Beginning 68 CE	
21.	Bowl base	Beginning 68 CE	
22.	Blue spindle whorl	68–96 CE	Havernick 1972
23.	Amphorisque	Late 1st–early 2nd century CE	

of this type of vessel along with a deposit of raw material for their manufacture.[34]

While not specifically indicating the diagnostic pieces, the glass map does mirror what we see from other types of finds. Figure 4.13 and its accompanying table show the diagnostic pieces that have been clearly identified. One rather surprising observation from the map, though, is the dearth of later Roman glass finds associated with the northern large courtyard houses. Both Dr. Rottloff and Dr. Fortner comment that this, for them, is an indication that these houses may have been abandoned during the later Roman occupation.[35] Also, one can note the concentration of occupation into the first, second, and third centuries CE in the central area above the Iron Age palace-gate complex. Architectural evidence, discussed below, points in the same direction, namely that the site may actually shrink in size from a Seleucid period peak.

STONE VESSELS

During the 2000 season at Bethsaida many interesting and important finds were uncovered relevant to our topic. Among them is a collection of limestone vessel fragments, which are important indicative pieces for Jewish presence in the Roman period. Aviam has identified eight categories of objects that can serve as definite ethnic markers for first century Jews or Christians.[36] At Bethsaida we have discovered examples of five of his eight categories of objects held to be indicative of Jewish presence in particular: Galilean Coarse Ware, Hasmonean coins, stone vessels, Kefar Hannania ware, including the "Galilean bowl," and possibly a secret hideaway. Noteworthy in this regard is that missing from the Bethsaida material record are miqvot, ossuaries, and synagogues.[37] However, from among the eight markers that Aviam details, one has been singled out as especially significant for late Second Temple Judaism. Yitzhak Magen describes the significance:

> Unlike other elements of the Jewish material culture during the Second Temple period, such as pottery, wooden, metal and glass vessels

and other implements that were conceived in previous periods and that remained a part of the material culture after the destruction of the Temple, chalk vessels are the only components of the material culture that appear suddenly in the late first century BCE and vanish after the destruction of the Second Temple and the Bar Kochba Revolt, without remaining in use and without returning to the material culture of the Land of Israel in succeeding periods.[38]

This marker is that of limestone or chalk vessels that were employed briefly during the time prior to the destruction of the Second Temple in 70 CE, perhaps continuing into the early second century CE.[39]

THE VESSELS OF BETHSAIDA

While there had been several discoveries of this type of vessel prior to the 2000 season—one in 1994, one in 1997, and another in 1998—during the 2000 season fragments of three such vessels were discovered in a relatively small area. These three vessels were discovered in Area A behind the Iron Age II gate complex in the early Roman strata above the Iron Age levels. These vessels are located within ten meters of the large structure that has been variously identified as a Roman era temple or possibly a "synagogual type" building.[40]

In locus 403, where the largest of the three recently discovered fragments was found, several Roman period pits filled with largely intact pottery were also discovered. One of these pits from the 2000 season is most likely a continuation of a pit first uncovered in 1999 that produced three nearly intact Roman period jugs. This suggests the possibility that the area was a place where vessels with some cultic significance were carefully disposed of after they were no longer eligible for use in religious service. The largest of the three limestone vessel fragments is a significant portion of a hand tooled limestone or chalk bowl. Locus 403 became known by the volunteers who worked this square as "the gold mine," since so many significant finds from the Early Roman period were uncovered there. This type of stone bowl is designated as "flat-based bowl with straight sides."[41] The vessel type is noted for the fluted effect that the chiseled sides of the bowl create. The vessels are hand carved, faceted, and polished smooth. They have straight sides and are always taller than they are wide. Most often this bowl has one of two types of handle: either a rectangular "lug" handle near the center of the bowl, or a bar handle near the rim. Since we are missing the rim and a significant portion of the body, our vessel may be of either of these sub-types or may be an example of the slightly less common flat-based bowl with straight sides and without handle. Parallel examples have been found in Jerusalem by Mazar, Magen, Avigad, and others.[42] In addition, this type of bowl has been found at Ramat Rahel, Bethany, Shiloh, Ashdod, and Hizma.[43] All of these examples were discovered in first century CE Jewish contexts.

A second fragment, in much poorer condition, was found in locus 405. This find is a body shard from a somewhat larger vessel than the hand chiseled bowls or mugs. We can note that it appears not to be a hand carved vessel since we do not see any of the characteristic chisel marks or flattened sides, but its type is less certain. Judging by the size and curvature, however, we can presume that it is a shard from a jar wall.[44] This type of jar is turned on a large lathe and is usually very tall and has a deep round base. Often they are footed. These vessels often had decorative motifs executed on their rims and sides, as found in Jerusalem and many of the same areas as before, although our small shard had no trace of such decoration.

The third indicative find from 2000, discovered in locus 423, was a barrel-shaped jar. All examples of this type of jar have large, open mouths with stepped, internal profiles. They were apparently intended to be lidded. They have broad rims, often sculpted, and may be either triangular or triple ridged, as in our example. They sometimes bear a decorative motif but are often undecorated. Jars and jar fragments of this type, undecorated and having a triple-ridged rim, have been found in Jerusalem around the Temple Mount, in the Jewish Quarter, at the Citadel, along the western slopes of Mount Zion and in the City of David. Outside of Jerusalem, however, this type is rare, previously only cited as being found at Hizma, from a workshop located in the central hill country.[45] Thus, our shard may be of significant importance.

Two of the three limestone vessels discovered at Bethsaida prior to 2000 were fragments of the lathe-turned type, with the third vessel being hand produced. The find from 1998 (locus 254) consists of three fragments of the same stone bowl, which would have had an opening at the top of approximately 19cm.[46] It is a lathe-turned vessel but turned on a small lathe as opposed to a large lathe such as that which would have been used for the jars described above from loci 405 and 423. This type of bowl has been designated by Magen as bowl type I, spherical vessels with low disk bases and slightly inverted hole-mouth rims.[47] Two closely spaced incised lines encircle the external wall just below the rim. The vessel lacks handles or any decorative motif other than the lines. These are the "mass produced" variety of chalk or limestone vessel. This vessel was not handcrafted, but instead was turned on a small lathe and smoothly milled to produce a very fine appearance that originally may have been designed to mimic the alabaster ware used in other religious contexts. For example, Egyptian temple and funerary practice often employed alabaster vessels of various types. While only a small piece from such a vessel was found at Bethsaida, the lines below the rim are very indicative. This type of vessel is very common in Jerusalem as well as in Bethany, Qalandiya, Shiloh, Samaria, Capernaum, Jericho, Herodian, and in the Wadi Murabba`at.[48]

The vessel fragment found in 1994 (locus 940) is the only one to come from Area C,[49] and it may perhaps be a fragment of a lathe-turned basin or jar. The depression in the rim may indicate that the vessel had employed a lid. Because of the uncertainty of identification of the vessel typology, however, it is not possible to cite parallels to this very fragmentary shard.

The final vessel to be discussed was found in 1997. It was handmade and is similar to the large bowl shard found in 2000. As with the 2000 find, the fragment included only a segment of the base and a small portion of a side. Because of the deteriorated condition of the 1997 find, it was not possible to determine whether or not the side originally had the faceting that is characteristic of this type of vessel, but it is nonetheless likely to have been the same type of bowl as the one found in 2000 (locus 403), though somewhat smaller. The base is only slightly more than 3 cm in diameter as compared to slightly more than 4 cm for the base found in 2000.

The total number of chalk vessel fragments seems low relative to the other finds at Bethsaida. Two factors argue against this being unexpected. First, several lime pits were found in Area C and the fact that the one vessel found in that area was discovered near one of these kiln pits suggests that at some period the site was "mined" for its available limestone. Second, the vulnerability of the soft material to weathering in the wet climate, combined with the fact that the Roman layer is at most points itself the surface layer of the tell, serve to negatively affect the survival of any chalk vessels. Many "lumps" of soft limestone material were found in a number of loci in Areas A, B, and C, "lumps" that cannot be unequivocally determined to be from chalk vessels but may in fact be badly weathered remnants.[50]

A subsequent search of all of the recovered diagnostic pottery shards from 1987 to 1999 led to the recognition of an additional four fragments of stoneware vessels similar to the types described above.[51] The vessels have been found in Areas A, B, and C—that is, in all the first century CE occupation areas of the excavated site. During the 2005 and 2007 dig seasons four additional fragments were also recovered in the same general area, A West, as the 2000 finds.

It should be noted as well that there are significant numbers of basalt vessels, much more numerous than limestone vessels, which were found in all areas of Bethsaida. These too would have the same qualities for ritual purity as the chalk vessels and may have been more likely to be locally produced since Bethsaida is replete with basalt. But, basalt vessels are for the most part undatable except by context and even so appear throughout all periods of occupation of Et-Tell/Bethsaida, that is both during the Iron Age settlement prior to the Assyrian conquest, and during the Hellenistic occupation of Bethsaida. Therefore they cannot serve as time sensitive ethnic indicators for the population that inhabited the site. Basalt vessels are used by all population groups throughout the area in all of the periods relevant to our investigation.

SIGNIFICANCE

If scholars are correct in their valuation of limestone ware as a marker for Jewish presence at a site, the value of finding such vessels at Bethsaida[52] cannot be underestimated. They could be the best indicators that we have of a possible first century CE Jewish community at Bethsaida. They are known to have been used at over fifty-nine different sites located throughout Roman period Judah with their peak occurrence in Jerusalem. Their popularity seems to have culminated in the period just prior to the Roman destruction of Jerusalem in 70 CE and then continued, according to some scholars, in smaller proportion through the period of the Bar Kochba revolt until abruptly ceasing in the mid second century CE.

Their presence at Bethsaida indicates a Jewish presence in the first century CE. Whether or not this Jewish presence would include early Christians, however, cannot be determined by this criterion alone.

ARCHITECTURE

The chronology of the late Hellenistic and early Roman periods at Bethsaida is problematic because of the fact that both levels are frequently located in the surface level, which has been eroded and disturbed by modern military occupation. Therefore, the settlement pattern of first century CE Bethsaida is only fragmentarily recognizable. It is often nearly impossible to distinguish between the latest Hellenistic and early Roman occupation levels. In recent years much more careful attention has been paid to this stratification problem, but the difficulty remains. However, an architectural redevelopment following the Iron Age destruction of the tell can be detected. In the northern part of the tell in Area B and C, two almost complete large courtyard houses along with several other nearby Hellenistic structures have been uncovered. While no overall rectilinear pattern street grid has been discovered, which is typical

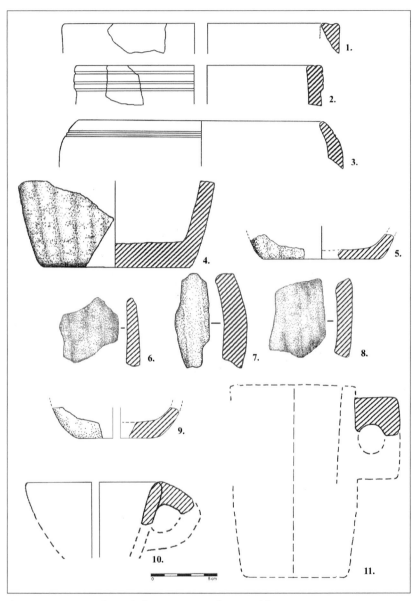

Figure 4.14. Drawings of Limestone Vessels (see table 4.6)
Source: DreAnna Hadash, Bethsaida Staff Artist

Table 4.6. Limestone Vessels

	Description	Area: Locus: Basket:	Date Found	Decoration	Parallels
1.	Rim shard-lathed vessel	C 940 9306	06-06-1994	Top groove on rim	
2.	Rim shard-lathed vessel	A 423 5966	05-07-2000	Top groove & three grooves on outside rim	Qedem 33 18:8
3.	Rim shard-small-lathed vessel	A 254 4015	11-06-1998	Two grooves at rim	Qedem 13, Herodium 11:8 Qedem 33 16.3
4.	Base shard-chiseled vessel	A 403 5685	29-05-2000	Soft chalky limestone	Qedem 13, Herodium 11:3
5.	Base shard-chiseled vessel	A 255 7048	26-06-1997	Soft chalky limestone	Qedem 13, Herodium
6.	Body shard-chiseled vessel	AI Surface	07-07-2005	Soft chalky limestone	Qedem 13, Herodium

Table 4.6. Limestone Vessels (*continued*)

	Description	Area: Locus: Basket:	Date Found	Decoration	Parallels
7.	Body shard-chiseled vessel	A 405 5716	01-06-2000	Soft chalky limestone	Qedem 13, Herodium
8.	Body shard-chiseled vessel	A 2001 18015	07-07-2005	Soft chalky limestone	Qedem 13, Herodium
9.	Base shard-chiseled vessel	A 1539 16012	11-06-2004	Soft chalky limestone	Qedem 33 20:10, Herodium
10.	Handle shard-chiseled vessel	A 254 #55N	11-06-1998	Soft chalky limestone	Qedem 33 20:7, Herodium pg 255 #7
11.	Handle shard-chiseled vessel	A West 2039 18330	20-06-2007	Soft chalky limestone	Qedem 13, Herodium Pl 11 pg 128 #4-5 Tel Dor pg 251, Qedem 33 20:4

of classic Hellenistic city planning, the road pattern may show some signs of orthogonal planning.[53]

In the southern part of Area B and in Area A, several Hellenistic-Roman structures appear to have reused parts of the Iron Age features, including walls, parts of rooms, and stone floors. An east-west oriented housing complex and possible Temple, along with a two-room house, are among these architectural features. It is clear from the two-room house that Iron Age walls and surfaces were often re-employed in the Hellenistic period.[54] It, like many buildings, incorporated the remnants of the outer city wall, the Bit-Hilani palace, and other Iron Age elements that must have been preserved and exposed during the Roman period.

Further, the now more than 100 meters of exposed roadway leading north from outside the Iron Age gate complex indicates reuse of the Iron Age roadbed in the later period. It seems that it was simply uncovered, needing neither major repair nor resurfacing. The substructure for the roadway, however, was clearly Iron Age construction. In a probe of the roadbed of about two by two meters conducted by the author in 2004, Hellenistic-Roman shards were found directly on top of the cobblestone of the road surface. Several of those shards had even migrated between the stones to become embedded in the packed earth between and immediately below the road surface. Only when the subfloor foundation was examined was it determined that the roadway was indeed an Iron Age construction that was reused in the later period. The paving stones were removed and the stratification of material below their surface carefully noted and analyzed. This was done to understand the relation between the Roman use and the Iron Age construction of the road system. The roadway is clearly connected to the Iron Age gate complex. The level of the surface, the size of cobbles, and the construction pattern match the inner courtyard and passageway of the Iron Age gate. Yet the pottery found on the road surface was just as clearly Roman/Hellenistic. Further, at several points in the roadway, intrusions into the road were made that disturbed the cobblestone pavement. Most notably among these were the more than five burials in the roadway. The graves are not well dated since almost no pottery was found in

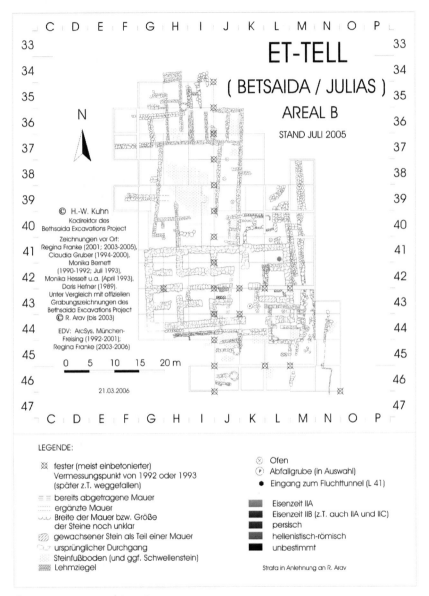

Figure 4.15. Map of Area B
Source: Professor emeritus Dr. Heinz-Wolfgang Kuhn, Ludwig-Maximilians-Universität München

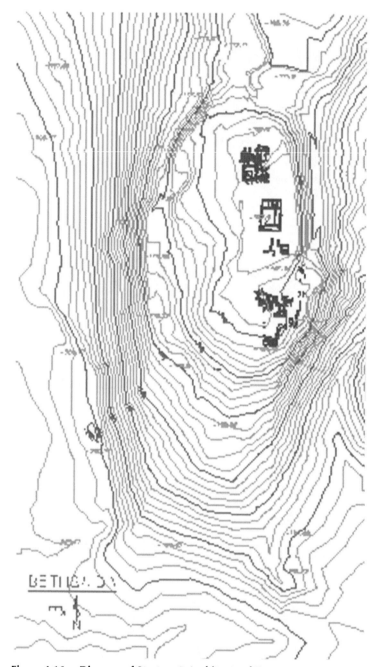

Figure 4.16. Diagram of Stratum 2 Architectural Features
Source: Dr. Rami Arav, Bethsaida Director of Excavations, University of Nebraska at Omaha

the partially sealed tombs, which were devoid of other grave goods.[55] However, it is likely that these were not Iron Age burials. The style of burial may in fact be most indicative of the "Qumran-type" burials found in the Qumran cemetery, single body shaft inhumation with north-south orientation from the Hellenistic period. This type of burial has a parallel in the Hellenistic Ptolemais cemetery as well.[56] Yet, while it is clear that there was extensive reuse of earlier remaining architectural remnants from the Iron Age during the Hellenistic reoccupation, and that some reuse of the road is clear, the roadway's connection to the Hellenistic/Roman city plan remains to be resolved as more of the outer later city is explored.

During the past five seasons, 2002 to 2007, I have been working just south of the "temple" building and just north of the building where the limestone vessels were found in 2000. In 2003 we were able to clearly identify the third century CE layer in that area. Ceramics indicative of the late second or third century CE and four coins clearly dated to the mid third century CE were found—pointing to the latest occupation stratum at Bethsaida. Beneath that layer we identified a second layer as second century CE, again with appropriate ceramics and two datable coins. The quality of construction in those loci mirrored what had been observed in other loci. Namely, the Roman walls were generally poorer in construction than the much grander Hellenistic buildings.

Thus, we note significant amounts of new construction at Bethsaida in the Hellenistic/Roman period. However, significant public buildings and features, such as a marketplace as found in Capernaum or Magdala, have not as yet been identified at Bethsaida. So, while we have the size and extent of a significant first century settlement, we cannot yet point to the typical large public institutions one associates with such a settlement.

OIL LAMPS

Because of their characteristic forms and recognizable patterns of seriation, oil lamps often provide an additional time marker. At

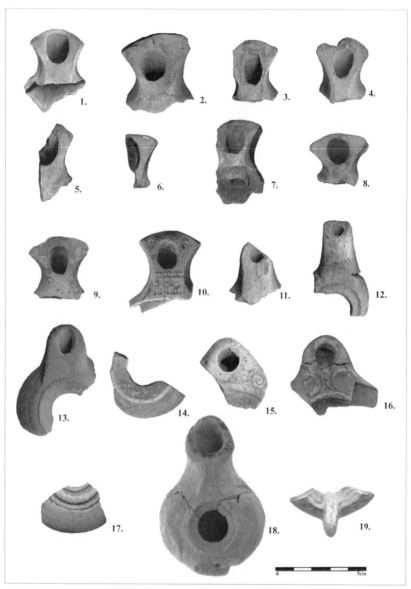

Figure 4.17.   Photographs and Scans of First Century Oil Lamps
Source: Carl E. Savage

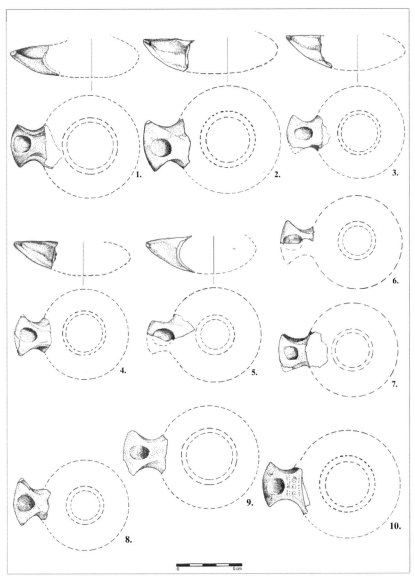

Figure 4.18.   Drawings of Herodian Oil Lamps (see table 4.7)
Source: DreAnna Hadash, Bethsaida Staff Artist

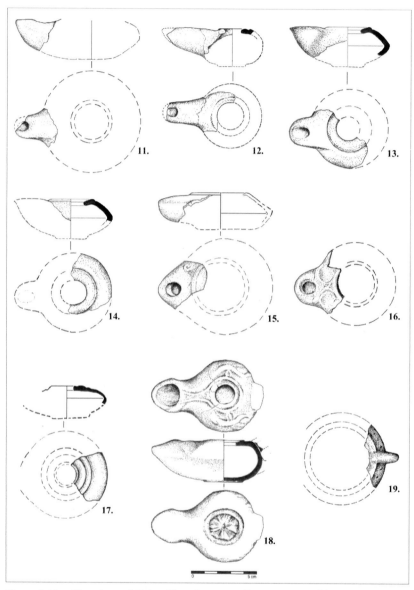

Figure 4.19.   Drawings of Other First Century Oil Lamps (see table 4.8)
Source: DreAnna Hadash, Bethsaida Staff Artist

Table 4.7. Herodian Oil Lamps

	Period	Area: Locus: Basket:	Clay Colors using Munsell	Construction/or evidence of burning	Parallels
1.	Herodian	A 526 1726	Color: 2.5YR 6/6 light red Surface burnished	Knife-pared nozzle	Qedem 8, p. 81 Meiron, p. 227
2.	Herodian	B 427	Color: 2.5YR 6/6 light red Surface burnished	Knife-pared nozzle	Qedem 8, p. 81 Meiron, p. 227
3.	Herodian	A 831 2947	Color: 10YR 7/6 yellow Surface burnished	Knife-pared nozzle	Qedem 8, p. 81 Meiron, p. 227
4.	Herodian	A 1508 16335	Color: 7.5YR 7/4 pink Surface burnished	Knife-pared nozzle with some burning at wick hole	Qedem 8, p. 81 Meiron, p. 227
5.	Herodian	A-West 2033 18280	Color: 10YR 7/6 yellow Surface burnished	Knife-pared nozzle with some burning at wick hole	Qedem 8, p. 81 Meiron, p. 227
6.	Herodian	B 444 5423	Color: 2.5 8/6 yellow Surface burnished	Knife-pared nozzle	Qedem 8, p. 81 Meiron, p. 227
7.	Herodian	A 831 2947	Color: NA Surface burnished	Knife-pared nozzle	Qedem 8, p. 81 Meiron, p. 227
8.	Herodian	B 18355 Locus 2035	Color: 5YR 6/3 light reddish brown Surface burnished	Knife-pared nozzle	
9.	Herodian	B18351 Locus 2035	Color: 7.5 YR 7/4 pink Surface burnished	Knife-pared nozzle	
10.	Herodian	C Roman house	Color: NA	Five stamped circles and three rows of dots	Qedem 8, p. 81 Meiron, p. 227

Table 4.8. Other First Century Oil Lamps

Period	Area: Locus: Basket:	Clay Colors using Munsell	Notes	Parallels
11. Late Hellenistic	B 20015 L11701	Color: 10YR 7/4 very pale brown	Crudely constructed; Undecorated 150–30 BCE	Meiron p226
12. Late Hellenistic	A 1513 16365	Color: 7.5YR 6/6 reddish yellow Slip: 10R 7/3 very pale brown	Grooved fill hole Wheel thrown undecorated	Qedem 8, fig 322
13. Late Helenistic?	B 303 2026	Color: 2.5 YR 5/6 red wheel thrown/highly fired	Wide inward sloping fill hole, much burning at wick hole undecorated	Araba 32.B, 50–150 CE Qedem 8, 324, form used into Byzantine period
14. Herodian	B 433 4392	Color: 7.5YR 6/6 reddish yellow slip: 5YR 4/6 yellowish red low fired	Wide inward sloping fill hole	Qedem 13 Ill. 93:1–1

Table 4.8. Other First Century Oil Lamps (*continued*)

	Period	Area: Locus: Basket:	Clay Colors using Munsell	Notes	Parallels
15.	Roman- Discus	A-South 807 2764	Color: 7.5YR 8/4 pink slip: 7.5YR 5/8 strong brown (traces) molded	Spiral design on nose, inward sloping thinned fill hole	Qedem 8, p. 85–89
16.	Roman-Discus	B 444 5422	Color: NA Slip: 2.5YR 4/8 red Molded (nearly covered)	Two disk shapes at nose with some burning at wick-hole	Qedem 8, p. 85–89 Araba, 32.G
17.	Roman-Discus	B 655 6064	Color: 7.5YR 6/6 reddish yellow Slip: 2.5YR 4/8 red molded (traces)	Three concentric circles radiating from the fill hole	Qedem 22, 129–130
18.	Nabatean type	A 216 3648	Color: NA	Decoration on top and center of base rim/missing handle/some burning at wick hole 1st century CE	Qedem 22, 1163–1165
19.	Roman	A K58 819-2853	Color: NA	Handle with some upper body	Qedem 8, p. 96

Bethsaida, we have a good sequence of oil lamps from the late Hellenistic into the first century CE. Herodian styles are clearly present as are later first century CE types. Well over two dozen oil lamp indicatives have been recovered for the first century CE.

The lamps of the Herodian type are variously dated but begin roughly at 37 BCE and continue until at least 70 CE. Herodian lamps typically have a rounded wheel-made body with a nozzle that was made separately and then attached to the body. The join between the body and spout was smoothed with a knife giving it a splayed shape, usually with concave sides. The term "knife-pared" lamp is an alternative designation given to this lamp and may be applied more appropriately since the lamp form seems to extend in time beyond the Herodian kingdom. The lamps are normally not decorated. One variation of this typical nondecorated form has four small circles and lines incised on the nozzle (see figure 4.17:10). Decorated Herodian lamps made from black clay are typical of the vicinity of Jerusalem and are, therefore, sometimes called "Jerusalem lamps." The aforementioned example, figure 4.17:10, may indeed be of such a type. The other common first century CE lamp found at Bethsaida is the Roman round lamp characterized by a sunken discus and round nozzle. Figures 4.17:15 and 4.17:16 are of this type and appear from the second half of the first century to the third century CE. A final first century type appears in figure 4.17:18 and may be of a "Nabatean-type." This form, perhaps a degenerative "factory made" type, can be found in various places in the empire of local manufacture. It typically is dated to the first century CE.[57]

CERAMICS

The pottery at Bethsaida shows a change from coastal import styles to a more local variety in the first centuries BCE/CE. For example, we have early forms of Eastern Sigillata A (ESA) but not later forms. There is evidence of local Galilean ware in the Roman period. Specifically, this means that the Galilean bowl and the everted rim casserole are very common components of the Early Roman pottery assemblage at Bethsaida. Most forms of local wares, such as the Kefar Shikhin and Kefar Hanania types, are found.[58]

Following David Adan-Bayewitz's work on the types of Kefar Hananya ware, we have identified a significant number of examples of most types in his taxonomy. While the discoveries have not yet been quantified according to his grid, we have present forms 1A, particularly type 4, 1C, 1B, 1D, 1E, 3A, 3B, 4B, 4C, 5A, 5B1, 6B, and 6C. We have no examples of Form 2 that I have been able to recognize in the record, though there are possible examples of Forms 4D, 4E, and perhaps 6A. It seems that Bethsaida does not yield any examples of the latest fifth century CE forms of Kefar Hananya ware. In terms of Adan-Bayewitz's chronological outline of the pottery forms, the sequence at Bethsaida seems to end with the forms that were introduced in the first decades of the fourth century CE.[59] This is consistent with the suggested timeline for Bethsaida's cessation as an occupied site, which is before the advent of the Byzantine period—and the precise terminus of occupation is not pertinent to this study. By far, the most common form from the Adan-Bayewitz typology is type 3A. The everted rim casserole is found in nearly every first century CE context across the site. Figure 4.25 shows a typical assemblage found in the Roman house in Area B of the tell.

Figures 4.20 to 4.23 indicate other pottery forms from the first century CE that are commonly found at Bethsaida.[60] When these forms appear in the assemblage, they are not found with any ESA or other imported ware in concurrent usage elsewhere in the Eastern Empire. That is, we do not find other pottery in use alongside undecorated locally produced Galilean ware typified in Adan-Bayewitz's study. This is a dramatic difference in the material assemblage at Bethsaida as compared to non-Jewish sites where they do find more common Roman types in their assemblage.[61]

As one progresses from the first century CE into the second and third centuries CE, however, there is again a presence of imported ware. This may be indicative of an influx of non-Jewish presence. Uzi Leibner notes that during the mid Roman period, which he delineates as 135–250 CE, there may have been as much as a 15 percent population growth in previously settled areas.[62] This prosperity is

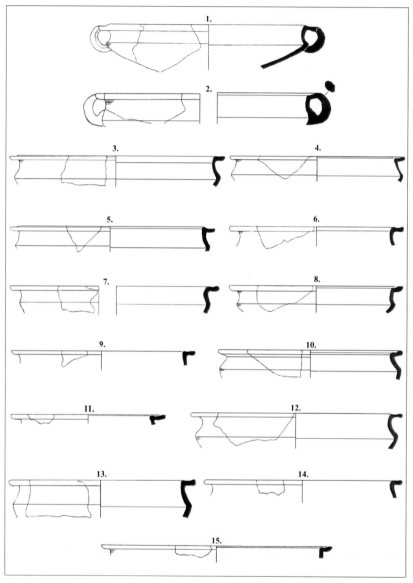

Figure 4.20. Drawings of Type 3A Everted Rim Casseroles (see table 4.9)
Source: Dr. Sandra Fortner, University of Munich, and DreAnna Hadash, Bethsaida Staff Artist

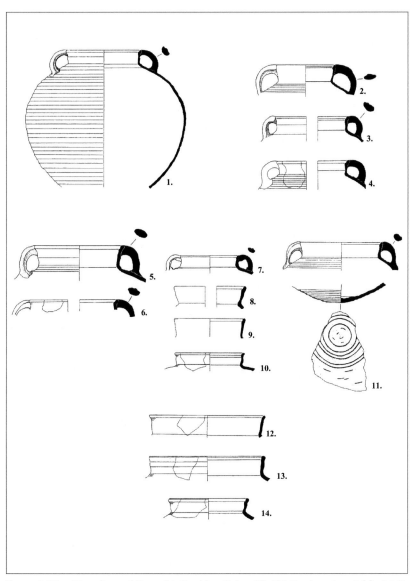

Figure 4.21. Drawings of Type 4A Cooking Pots with Lid Devices (see table 4.10)
Source: Dr. Sandra Fortner, University of Munich, and DreAnna Hadash, Bethsaida Staff Artist

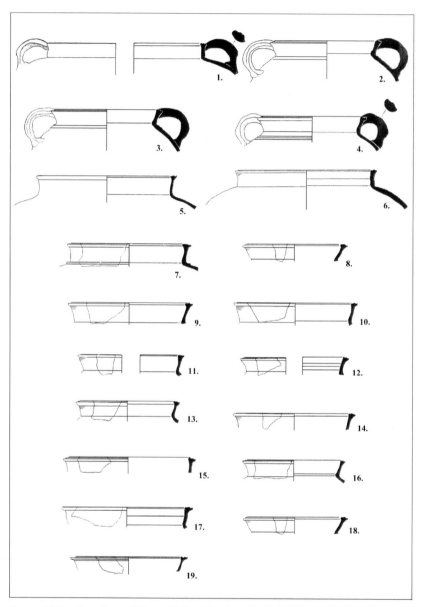

Figure 4.22.   Drawings of Type 4B Cooking Pots (see table 4.11)
Source: Dr. Sandra Fortner, University of Munich, and DreAnna Hadash, Bethsaida Staff Artist

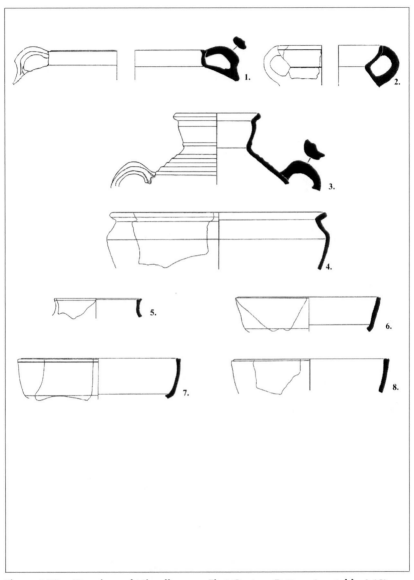

Figure 4.23. Drawings of Miscellaneous First Century Pottery (see table 4.12)
Source: Dr. Sandra Fortner, University of Munich, and DreAnna Hadash, Bethsaida Staff Artist

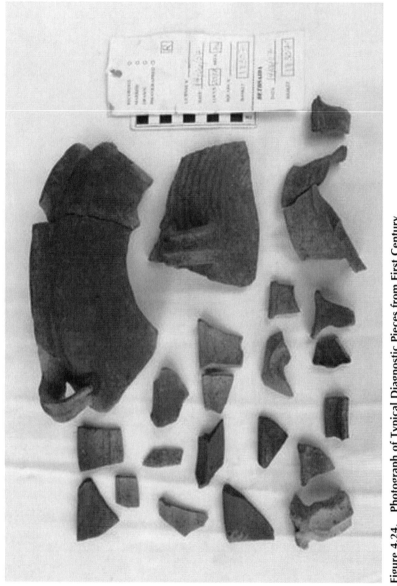

Figure 4.24.   Photograph of Typical Diagnostic Pieces from First Century
Source: Hanan Shafir, Ramat Hasharon, Israel, Bethsaida Staff Photographer 2006–present

Figure 4.25. Photograph of Assemblage of Cooking Ware
Source: Christine Dalenta, Bethsaida Staff Photographer

Figure 4.26. Photograph of Assemblage of Jugs and Jars from Roman Pit
Source: Christine Dalenta, Bethsaida Staff Photographer

Figure 4.27. Photograph of Late Hellenistic/Early Roman Storage Jars
Source: Christine Dalenta, Bethsaida Staff Photographer

found in sites such as Sepphoris and Meiron as they expand greatly from their early second century CE sizes.[63]

At Meiron they note that the material culture elements, particularly the ceramic and numismatic evidence, "form a picture of a burgeoning population" during the middle Roman period.[64] They suggest that the favorable conditions for growth are the product of the relative peace enjoyed under the Severan emperors. It may be that we witness the same phenomenon at Bethsaida.[65]

FAUNAL EVIDENCE

Dr. Toni Fisher, zooarchaeologist for the Bethsaida Excavations Project consortium, in her analysis of the faunal remains from the late Hellenistic/early Roman occupational strata, has made some interesting observations that fit with the suggested pattern. Namely, she notes a paucity of pig bones in the material record for this period. In

Table 4.9. Type 3A Everted Rim Casseroles

	Description	Dates	Area: Locus: Basket:	Special Features	Parallels
1. R182	Casserole with carinated body		L450	One handle present see figure 4.24 for a similar vessel	Gamla 2.18, 2
2. R19		100BCE–100 CE		Nearly vertical horizontal rim	Gamla 2.18, 4
3. R183	Kefar Hananya 3a cooking vessel with deep open container, rounded shoulders and rim that is inwardly concave to nearly flat	Mid 1st century BCE to mid 2nd century CE	Roman house located in area B square L/M 44–45 see figure 4.15.	These are common types in all Roman period loci. Recently more were uncovered in A west loci 2026, 2027	Gamla 2.16, 12–14 Meiron 8.11, 22–29 (although they are called bowls in the plate)
4. R184	Same as #3				
5. R185	Same as #3				
6. R186	Same as #3				
7. R187	Same as #3				
8. R188	Same as #3				
9. R22	Same as #3				
10. R190	Same as #3				Gamla 2.16, 13
11. R23	Same as #3				
12. R192	Same as #3				
13. R20	Same as #3				
14. R191	Same as #3				
15. R189	Same as #3				

Table 4.10. Type 4A Cooking Pots with Lid Devices

	Description	Dates	Area: Locus: Basket:	Special Features	Parallels
1.	Cooking pot with single groove in rim. These have been found in the Galilee at Capernaum, Meiron, Gamla	15–150 CE	Found mainly in Areas A and B.	Probably used with lids with the groove serving to stabilize the lid	Tel Anafa PW 207 Gamla 2.14, 2.15 Meiron Plate 6.1, 1–6 Loffreda Plate 2
2.	Same as #1	15–50 CE			Tel Anafa PW 197; Gamla 2.10 #1
3.	Same as #1				
4.	Same as #1				
5.	Same as #1				Tel Anafa PW212
6.	Same as #1				
7.	Same as #1				Tel Anafa PW178
8.	Same as #1				
9.	Same as #1				
10	Same as #1				
11.	Same as #1				Gamla 2.12 #3
12.	Same as #1				
13.	Same as #1				
14.	Same as #1				

Table 4.11. Type 4B Cooking Pots

	Description	Dates	Area: Locus: Basket:	Special Features	Parallels
1.	Cooking pot with double grooved rim type 4B using Adan-Bayewitz's typology	50 CE–100 CE		Neck almost vertical	Capernaum Loffreda Plate 3.1; Nazereth Bagatti Plate 17.5; Gadera Plate 11.6; Diez-Fernandez p 155; Gamla p. 40; Tel Anafa PW216–18
2.	Same as #1				Adan-Bayewitz 4B:2
3.	Same as #1				
4.	Same as #1				
5.	Same as #1				Adan-Bayewitz 4B:2
6.	Same as #1			Neck almost vertical	
7.	Same as #1				Tel Anafa PW 216
8.	Same as #1				Adan-Bayewitz 4B:3
9.	Same as #1				
10.	Same as #1				Adan-Bayewitz 4b:1
11.	Same as #1				Adan-Bayewitz 4b:2
12.	Undetermined				
13.	Undetermined				Adan-Bayewitz 4b:2
14.	Undetermined				Adan-Bayewitz 4b:2
15.	Undetermined				
16.	Undetermined				Adan-Bayewitz 4b:2
17.	Undetermined				
18.	Undetermined				
19.	Undetermined				

Table 4.12. Miscellaneous Pottery

	Description	Dates	Area: Locus: Basket:	Special Features	Parallels
1.	Cooking pot with double ridged rim	50–150 CE	B 460		
2.	Globular cooking pot		B		
3.	Jar with everted rim	50–250 CE	B 460		Tel Anafa PW 473
4.	Bowl with everted rim		B		
5.	Cooking pot with deep groove in rim	50 BCE–50 CE	B 610		Kefar Hananya
6.	Dish with simply grooved rim	60–200 CE	B 460		Loffreda 1974 #36; Fernandez 1983 126.214; Adan-Bayewitz 88–91
7.	Dish with simply grooved rim	60–200 CE	B 460		Loffreda 1974 #36; Fernandez 1983 126.214
8.	Dish with simply grooved rim	60–200 CE	B 460		Loffreda 1974 #36; Fernandez 1983 126.214

fact, she notes that in Area B no pig bones were found in the six loci that she examined. In other loci the percentage never rises above 3 percent and the bones recovered do not seem to indicate that the pigs were used for meat.[66] This compares with a ratio of nearly 5:1 pigs to caprids at Tel Anafa during the Roman period.[67] Tel Anafa is thought to be a non-Jewish site.[68] Andrea Berlin describes the settlers of early first century CE Tel Anafa as "Roman/Italic mercenaries of Herod Philip" on the basis of the implications of culinary taste through the identification of the ceramic corpus found at the settlement during the Early Roman period. She determines that the array of amphorae and varied cooking vessels indicate Roman tastes in food preparation and concern with food and drink, which point to settlement by soldiers who were "eminently practical and hardly self-indulgent" and who tend to be "quite concerned with food and drink."[69]

CONCLUSIONS

The evidence demonstrates that a first century CE settlement was in existence at Bethsaida. The archaeological evidence would suggest further that the settlement had declined somewhat from the late Hellenistic period, but that first century CE Bethsaida had incorporated elements of the larger Hellenistic settlement. The lack of destruction debris and the well sequenced numismatic evidence argues for a continuous settlement from the third century BCE on, although that is not completely clear. The first century CE Bethsaida appears to be less wealthy, no longer as oriented to the Phoenician coast, and more oriented to the west and south—the Jewish Galilee—than the earlier Hellenistic period settlement. Further, in terms of its ethnic identity, it shows elements of being predominantly a Jewish rather than a Gentile settlement.

NOTES

1. Chancey, *The Myth of a Gentile Galilee: The Population of Galilee and New Testament Studies*, 27.

2. Chancey, *The Myth of a Gentile Galilee: The Population of Galilee and New Testament Studies*, 7.

3. Peters, *The Harvest of Hellenism a History of the Near East from Alexander the Great to the Triumph of Christianity*, 283.

4. Mordechai Aviam argues that "no mixed communities existed in the rural areas. Unlike cities, where a diversity of beliefs and faiths was very common, small villages were closed societies, especially during periods when deep antagonism existed." Aviam, *Jews, Pagans, and Christians in the Galilee: 25 Years of Archaeological Excavations and Surveys: Hellenistic to Byzantine Periods*, 20.

5. Our findings are consistent, for example, with Andrea Berlin's recently published study of the pottery of Gamla. Andrea M. Berlin, *Gamla I: The Pottery of the Second Temple Period, the Shmarya Gutmann Excavations, 1976–1989*, IAA Reports (Jerusalem: Israel Antiquities Authority, 2006). One could also look to more recent general surveys, such as that by Uzi Leibner. Uzi Leibner, "Settlement and Demography in Late Roman and Byzantine Eastern Galilee," in *Settlements and Demography in the Near East in Late Antiquity: Proceedings of the Colloquium, Matera, 27–29 October 2005*, ed. Ariel Lewin, Biblioteca di Mediterraneo Antico (Pisa: Istituti editoriali e poligrafici internazionali, 2006), 105–30.

6. In most details, my proposed time line seems to mirror Chancey's larger proposal for the whole of the Galilean area. However, I suspect that at some periods in its development Bethsaida did indeed have a significant "Greek" population. The evidence for this will be discussed later. Chancey, *The Myth of a Gentile Galilee: The Population of Galilee and New Testament Studies*, 28–62.

7. Segal gives a brief history of development at Hellenistic Sussita in his article in *Biblical Archaeology Review*. While the origins under the Ptolemies and conquest by the Seleucids parallel that of Bethsaida's history, Sussita differs in that in 83–80 BCE Alexander Janneaus conquered the city. This, as we shall see, is significantly later than what is proposed during the Hasmonean time period at Bethsaida. Later in 63 BCE the city became part of the province of Roman Syria. It was given to Herod in 37 BCE when his kingdom was established, but was returned to Syria at the request of the inhabitants following his death in 4 BCE. Segal notes that the literature supports the idea of a "Jewish minority" being present at Sussita and in its surrounding hub of settlements. This subsequent history differs significantly from that experienced at Bethsaida. Segal, "The Spade Hits Sussita," 43–45.

8. This is the current position of Dr. Rami Arav, directing archaeologist of the Bethsaida Excavations project, and others of the research team. Rami Arav, "Towards a Comprehensive History of Geshur," in *The Bethsaida Excavations Project Reports and Contextual Studies*, ed. Rami Arav (Kirksville, MO: Thomas Jefferson University Press, 2004), 15–16.

9. See table 4.1, Coin Frequency at Bethsaida by Dynasty, page 70.

10. In an article, Donald T. Ariel, "Stamped Amphora Handles from Bethsaida," in *The Bethsaida Excavations Project Reports and Contextual Studies, V 4*, ed. Rami. Arav (Kirksville, MO: Thomas Jefferson University Press, 2009), 269, Ariel states that "[t]he dates of the stamped handles suggest that Bethsaida was occupied beginning in the last third of the third century BCE." He notes that for him the coin evidence of some Ptolemy I coins [there are only four clearly identified] and a larger number of Ptolemy II coins are not indicative of a possible earlier occupation as these coins were likely still in circulation.

11. Jodi Magness, "Did Galilee Decline in the Fifth Century?" Ancient Galilee in Interaction: Religion, Ethnicity, and Identity (Yale University, 2004).

12. See table 4.2, Distribution of Bethsaida Coins by Ruler, page 71. The chart depicts by ruler the coins discovered at Bethsaida up to the first century CE. The chart does not include the many second and third century CE coins, nor the city coins from the Phoenician coast.

13. See the section in this chapter, "Ceramics," page 110, for a discussion of the changes in the ceramic assemblages.

14. Berlin, "The Hellenistic Period," 428.

15. Gérald Finkielsztejn, "Politique et Commerce à Rhodes au IIe s. a.C.: Le Témoignage Des Exportations d'Amphores," in Les Cités d'Asie Mineure Occidentale au IIe Siècle a.C (Bordeaux: Ausonius-Publications, 2001), 191.

16. Ptol. = Ptolemaic; Sel. = Seleucid; Has. = Hasmonean; City = coins from Phoenician coastal cities; Her. = Herodian; Rom. 1st = first century CE Roman coins.

17. Ariel, "Stamped Amphora Handles from Bethsaida," 270.

18. Syon and Yavor, "Gamla Old and New," 6.

19. There may be one exception in the small find record. A military-style pickax, a dolabra, was found in a Hellenistic context in Area C in a building west of the large courtyard houses known as the "wine maker's house" and the "fisherman's house." This area on the north end of the tell seems to be a primary area of resettlement activity in the third century BCE at Bethsaida.

20. There have been five identifiable Ptolemy I coins and three earlier Persian period coins. These are recorded by the author in the Bethsaida Excavations Coin database, having been identified by Dr. Arieh Kindler, project numismatist.

21. His coin analysis was incorporated in the Coin Database that I constructed, see Appendix 2, page 177.

22. See table 4.1, Coin Frequency at Bethsaida by Dynasty, page 70, and table 4.3, Coin Distribution by Century, page 72.

23. Ilan Shachar, "The Later Coinage of Alexander Jannaeus and Its Historical Implications," unpublished MA thesis (Tel Aviv University, 2002).

24. Yaakov Meshorer, *A Treasury of Jewish Coins: From the Persian Period to Bar Kokhba* (Nyack: Amphora, 2001), 38.

25. "The numismatic pattern at Bethsaida suggests that the city was abandoned towards the end of Jannaeus' reign and resettled late in the first century BCE." Shachar, "The Later Coinage of Alexander Jannaeus and Its Historical Implications," 59.

26. There are also significant numbers of indicative shards of amphora ware without handles being associated with them. These include both Rhodian and non-Rhodian type.

27. Ariel, "Stamped Amphora Handles from Bethsaida," 269.

28. Ariel, "Stamped Amphora Handles from Bethsaida," 269.

29. Ariel notes a connection made by Finkielsztejn (Finkielsztejn, "Politique et Commerce à Rhodes au IIe s. a.C.: Le Témoignage Des Exportations d'Amphores") between the remains of (wine) amphoras and a military presence. Thus, for him, the initial occupation could have been short-lived. He supports this conclusion with the observation that at Bethsaida there is very little handle evidence from the peak production period of Rhodian amphoras. Again citing this article by Finkielsztejn, Ariel notes that this peak period is well represented at other sites in the Southern Levant.

30. Ariel, "Stamped Amphora Handles from Bethsaida," 271.

31. The brief citations listed in table 4.4 refer to the following sources: Finkielstejn 2001a refers to Gérald Finkielsztejn, *Chronologie Détaillée et Révisée Des Éponymes Amphoriques Rhodiens, de 270 à 108 av. J.-C. Environ Premier Bilan* (Oxford, England: Archaeopress, 2001); Johrens 1999 refers to Gerhard Jöhrens, *Amphorenstempel Im Nationalmuseum von Athen zu Den von H.G. Lolling Aufgenommenen "Unedierten Henkelinschriften"* (Mainz: In Kommission bei P. von Zabern, 1999); Conovici and Irimia 1991 refers to N. Conovici and M. Irimia, "Timbres Amphoriques et Autres Inscriptions Céramiques Découverts à Satu Nou," *Dacia: Revue d'Archéologie et d'Histoire*

Ancienne 35 (1991): 139–75; Schuchhardt 1895 refers to Carl Schuchhardt, "Amphorenstempel," in *Die Inschriften von Pergamon 2, Römische Zeit-Inschriften auf Thon Altertümer von Pergamon VIII, 2* (Berlin: W. Spemann, 1895), 423–98; Borker 1998 refers to Christoph Börker, "Der Pergamon-Komplex," in *Die Hellenistischen Amphorenstempel Aus Pergamon* (Berlin, 1998), 3–69; Finkielstejn 2000 refers to Gérald Finkielsztejn, "Amphoras and Stamped Handles from 'Akko,'" *Atiqot: Journal of the Israel Department of Antiquities* 39 (2000): 135–53; Radulescu, Barbulescu and Buzoiana refers to A. Radulescu, M. Barbulescu, and L. Buzoianu, "Importuri Amforice la Albesti (Jud. Constanta): Rhodes," *Pontica* 20 (1987): 79–106.

32. See figure 4.12, Map of Glass Small Finds, page 88, and table 4.5, Small Glass Finds, page 90, which contains the descriptions and parallels. The brief citations in table 4.5 refer to the following: Avigad 1983 refers to Nahman Avigad, *Discovering Jerusalem* (Nashville: T. Nelson, 1983); Ariel 1990 (Jerusalem) refers to Donald T. Ariel, *Excavations at the City of David 1978–1985 Directed by Yigal Shiloh, Vol. II: Imported Stamped Amphora Handles, Coins, Worked Bone and Ivory, and Glass*, Qedem 30 (Jerusalem: Institute of Archaeology, Hebrew University of Jerusalem, 1990); Meyers et al. (Meiron) 1981 refers to Eric M. Meyers, James F. Strange, and Carol L. Meyers, *Excavations at Ancient Meiron, Upper Galilee, Israel, 1971–72; 1974–74, 1977* (Cambridge, MA: American Schools of Oriental Research, 1981); Davidson Weinberg (Tel Anafa) refers to G. D. Weinberg, "Hellenistic Glass from Tel Anafa in Upper Galilee," *Journal of Glass Studies* 12 (1970): 17–27; Isings refers to C. Isings, *Roman Glass from Dated Finds*, Archaeologica Traiectina (Groningen: J. B. Wolters, 1957); Havernick refers to Th. E. Havernick, "Nadelköpfe Vom Typ Kempten," *Germania* 50 (1972): 136–48.

33. Andrea Rottloff, "Hellenistic, Roman and Islamic Glass from Bethsaida (*Iulias*, Israel)," *Annuals of the 14th Congress of the International Association for the History of Glass* (2000) (Lochem, Netherlands: AIHV, 2000).

34. Rottloff, "Hellenistic, Roman and Islamic Glass from Bethsaida (*Iulias*, Israel)," 142–43.

35. Rottloff notes, "The Hellenistic period is represented by several courtyard buildings, which were abandoned in early Roman times." Rottloff, "Hellenistic, Roman and Islamic Glass from Bethsaida (*Iulias*, Israel)," 142. Presumably this observation was based on her small finds, but it could also be based on her following the early principle researchers' position that the site was abandoned following the great revolt of 70 CE. Taking the writings of Josephus as a reliable historical source one might have assumed such an abandonment following the unsuccessful skirmish with the

Romans near Bethsaida that is recorded in his *Life 70-71*. Flavius Josephus, *The Works of Flavius Josephus, Volume II*, trans. William Whiston (Nashville, TN: Baker Book House, 1974), 54–55

36. Aviam has identified various archaeological finds as particular ethnic or cultural markers. He cites as Jewish markers: Galilean Coarse Ware (GCW)–Jewish; Hasmonean coins; Miqvaot; stone vessels; Kefar Hannania ware, in particular the first century CE "Galilean bowl"; secondary burial in ossuaries; secret hideaways; and synagogues; as Roman or "pagan" markers: Phoenician Jar; human statues; temples; and as a Christian marker, although from a later period, churches. Mordechai Aviam, "Distribution Maps of Archaeological Data in the Galilee as an Attempt to Create Ethnic and Religion Zones," conference presentation, Ancient Galilee in Interaction: Religion, Ethnicity, and Identity (Yale University, 2004).

37. There has been debate among the researchers at Bethsaida concerning a large rectangular structure that has many features of an important public building. This structure has been variously called a pagan temple or a synagogue, but recent discussion has moved away from calling the building a synagogue. There is, however, a later third or fourth century synagogue located approximately 3 km NW of Bethsaida along the upper Jordan river at Khirbet ed-Dikkeh. Dan Urman, "The Public Structures and Jewish Communities in the Golan Heights," in *Ancient Synagogues Historical Analysis and Archaeological Data*, ed. Dan Urman and Paul V. M. Flesher, Studia Post-Biblica (Leiden and New York: E. J. Brill, 1995), 503–9.

38. Yitzhak Magen, *The Stone Vessel Industry in the Second Temple Period* (Jerusalem: Israel Exploration Society, 2002), 100.

39. Stuart S. Miller notes concerning stone vessels: "They are found largely at sites that we know, from either literary or archaeological courses—or both—were Jewish. This, it would seem, is convincing enough reason to assign to them the role of an identification marker denoting a Jewish site." Stuart S. Miller, "Some Observations on Stone Vessel Finds and Ritual Purity in Light of Talmudic Sources," in *Zeichen Aus Text und Stein*, Stefan Alkier and Jürgen Zangenberg (Tübingen: Francke Verlag, 2003), 403.

40. See Excursus 1 on the "Temple" of Bethsaida.

41. Magen, *The Stone Vessel Industry in the Second Temple Period*, 100.

42. Described by Magen as hand-carved mugs and bowls, even a "measuring cup," this type of vessel has been found over a wide area as noted by Magen in his Appendix I. Magen, *The Stone Vessel Industry in the Second Temple Period*, 167–73. Bethsaida can now be added to his list.

43. This type of vessel has been found at three Galilean sites: Capernaum, Stanislao Loffreda, *La Sinagoga di Cafarnao, Dopo Gli Scavi del 1969* (Jerusalem: Francescani, 1970); Meiron, Meyers, James F. Strange, and Carol L. Meyers, *Excavations at Ancient Meiron, Upper Galilee, Israel, 1971–72; 1974–74, 1977*; and Kefar Hananyah, David Adan-Bayewitz, "Kafr Hananya—1987," in *Excavations and Surveys in Israel 7–8* (Jerusalem: Israel Dept. of Antiquities and Museums, 1988/89).

44. Dr. James Strange suggested at a recent conference that perhaps I should consider whether it might be from a squared vessel. James F. Strange, Batchelder Biblical Archaeology Conference, conversation with the author, Batchelder Biblical Archaeology Conference (University of Nebraska at Omaha, 2004, 22–24 October).

45. Jane M. Cahill, "Chalk Vessel Assemblages of the Persian/Hellenistic and Early Roman Periods," *Qedem* 33 (1992): 208–9.

46. A fourth fragment of this same bowl was recovered by the author in January 2004 when checking the stored diagnostic pottery shards from the surrounding loci.

47. Magen, *The Stone Vessel Industry in the Second Temple Period*, 65. He notes that these are remarkably similar to terra sigillata, local pottery, and wooden vessels. Indeed, the author found one such wooden parallel in the Cave of Letters during the John and Carol Merrill Expedition in 2000.

48. See Magen, Appendix 1. Magen, *The Stone Vessel Industry in the Second Temple Period*, 167–73.

49. This observation may be significant since Area C is the location of the large courtyard houses that may represent the earliest occupation area for Bethsaida during the Hellenistic period. My suggestion is that the earliest settlers may have been for the most part colonists from the Ptolemaic coastal cities and that later occupation of these buildings may not have continued into the Roman period, as indicated by the glass finds.

50. In scrutinizing the daily pottery evaluation diaries and the saved diagnostic pieces in the lab at Bethsaida for chalk vessels, the author noted well over fifty pieces of limestone that were kept for diagnostic purposes. From among those, three could be recognized as distinct chalk vessel fragments that were previously missed as such. One of those was found to be an additional fragment of an already recognized vessel. As stated previously in footnote 45, that fragment matched the small lathe-turned bowl from locus 254 (1998). Many more notations of "limestone" finds were noted in the field diaries without the fragments being preserved. Not all

of these other fragments should be considered as from actual vessels, but some likely were.

51. A search of the items designated fishing net weights yielded another misidentified limestone vessel fragment; see figure 4.14:10, page 97.

52. Figure 4.14, Drawings of Limestone Vessels, and table 4.6, Limestone Vessels, contain the illustrations, descriptions, and parallels for these vessels. The brief citations in table 4.6 refer to the following: Qedem 33 refers to Jane M. Cahill, "Chalk Assemblages of the Persian/Hellenistic and Early Roman Periods," in *Qedem 33* (Jerusalem: Institute of Archaeology, Hebrew University of Jerusalem, 1992), 190–274; Qedem 13 refers to Ehud Netzer, *Greater Herodium*, Qedem 13 (Jerusalem: Institute of Archaeology, Hebrew University of Jerusalem, 1981); Tel Dor refers to Qedem 22 Avraham Negev, *The Late Hellenistic and Early Roman Pottery of Nabatean Oboda*, Qedem 22 (Jerusalem: Institute of Archaeology, Hebrew University of Jerusalem, 1986).

53. During the 2007 season a right angle corner to the street abutting the northernmost large courtyard house was unearthed.

54. See figure 4.15, Map of Area B, page 101. The two-room house is the structure in the lower right of the map. Note that it incorporates the Iron Age city wall as its eastern wall.

55. Most of the tombs recovered in the roadway were covered with large stretcher stones, but these did not form a complete seal over the graves and material would have been able to migrate into the body cavity.

56. Vasillios Tsaferis, "The Ancient Cemetery of Akko-Ptolemais," in *The Western Galilee Antiquities* (Tel Aviv, Israel: Misrad ha-bitahon ha-Moatsah ha-ezorit Mateh Asher, ha-Hug ha-ezori li-yedi at ha-Arets, 1986), 266 ff.

57. Figures 4.17–4.19 and tables 4.7–4.8 contain the illustrations, descriptions, and parallels for the oil lamps. The brief citations in the tables refer to the following: Qedem 8 refers to Renate Rosenthal and Renee Sivan, *Ancient Lamps in the Schloessinger Collection*, Qedem 8 (Jerusalem: Institute of Archaeology, Hebrew University of Jerusalem, 1978); Meiron refers to Meyers, James F. Strange, and Carol L. Meyers, *Excavations at Ancient Meiron, Upper Galilee, Israel, 1971–72;1974–74, 1977*; Araba refers to Edna J. Stern, "'Araba," *Excavations and Surveys in Israel* 18, no. 106 (1998): 15, (22–24 Heb.); Qedem 22 refers to Negev, *The Late Hellenistic and Early Roman Pottery of Nabatean Oboda*.

58. We have not discovered any pottery manufacturing facility at Bethsaida. So the term "local ware" is in some way misleading. It should per-

haps be more properly termed regional ware, as it is produced in the local region but not in the settlement.

59. His chronological sequence is laid out in his study of the Kefar Hananya repertoire. Adan-Bayewitz, *Common Pottery in Roman Galilee: A Study of Local Trade*, 83–154.

60. Tables 4.9–4.12, which accompany the pottery drawings, figures 4.20–4.23, use the following citations for parallels: Gamla refers to Berlin, *Gamla I: The Pottery of the Second Temple Period, the Shmarya Gutmann Excavations, 1976–1989*; Tel Anafa refers to Sharon C. Herbert, Leslie A. Cornell, Andrea M. Berlin, and Kathleen W. Slane, *The Hellenistic and Roman Pottery*, ed. Sharon C. Herbert, Tel Anafa (Ann Arbor, MI: Kelsey Museum of the University of Michigan, 1997); Meiron refers to Meyers, James F. Strange, and Carol L. Meyers, *Excavations at Ancient Meiron, Upper Galilee, Israel, 1971–72;1974–74, 1977*; Loffreda refers to Stanislao Loffreda, *Cafarnao 2: La Ceramica* (Jerusalem: Francescani, 1974); Nazareth refers to Bellarmino Bagatti, "Scavo Presso la Chiesa di San Giuseppe a Nazaret," *Liber Annuus* (1971); Gadera refers to F.G. Andersen and James F. Strange, "Bericht Über Drei Sondagen Im Umm Qais, Jordanien, Im Herbst 1983," *Zeitschrift Des Deutschen Palästina-Vereins* 103 (1987): 90–92, plate 11.6; Diez-Fernandez/Fernandez refers to Florentino Díez Fernández, *Cerámica Común Romana de la Galilea Aproximaciones y Diferencias con la Cerámica del Resto de Palestina y Regiones Circundantes* (Madrid: Ed. Biblia y Fé Escuela Bíblica, 1983); Adan-Bayewitz/Kefar Hananya refers to Adan-Bayewitz, *Common Pottery in Roman Galilee: A Study of Local Trade*.

61. See, for example, Tel Anafa: Herbert, Cornell, Berlin, and Slane, *The Hellenistic and Roman Pottery*; Pella: Robert Houston Smith and Leslie Preston Day, *Pella of the Decapolis* (Wooster, OH: College of Wooster, 1973); or Sussita: Arthur Segal, *Hippos-Sussita Fifth Season of Excavations: September–October 2004* (Haifa: Zinman Institute of Archaeology, University of Haifa, 2004).

62. He notes that this is a regional peak for population for Eastern Galilee. Leibner, "Settlement and Demography in Late Roman and Byzantine Eastern Galilee," 115–16.

63. An important development in the layout of Zippori occurred during the first half of the second century CE. It appears that by this time the hill and all of its slopes were completely built up; an increase in the population and the higher standard of living called for an extension of the city limits. The fairly level area (with a gentle slope toward the south) to the east of

the hill was suited for this purpose. This expansion was well planned. An area of at least five hectares was marked out and a street grid was constructed, giving rise to a series of insulae, or organized blocks of space. Z. Weiss and E. Netzer, "The Hebrew University Excavations at Sepphoris," Qadmoniot, 113 (1997), pp. 2–21.

64. Meyers, James F. Strange, and Carol L. Meyers, *Excavations at Ancient Meiron, Upper Galilee, Israel, 1971–72;1974–74, 1977*, 157.

65. However, after the mid-third century at Meiron, the growth and prosperity explodes in renewed construction and renovation. This is precisely the period when Bethsaida seems to be in the process of abandonment. Meyers, James F. Strange, and Carol L. Meyers, *Excavations at Ancient Meiron, Upper Galilee, Israel, 1971–72;1974–74, 1977*, 157.

66. Toni Fisher, "The Zooarchaeological Implications of et-Tel/Bethsaida from the Iron Age to Early Roman Periods," unpublished dissertation (Knoxville: University of Tennessee, 2005), 70–97.

67. Richard W. Redding, "The Vertebrate Fauna," in *Tel Anafa I*, Journal of Roman Archaeology (Ann Arbor: Kelsey Museum of the University of Michigan, 1994), 288–89. Tel Anafa is a "pagan" site. The ratio indicates a much higher presence of pig in the diet.

68. Both the presence of the pig bones and the presence of an Italian-style pan in the ceramic corpus lead the excavators to suggest that perhaps even Roman settlers occupied the site during the first half of the first century. Mark A. Chancey and Adam L. Porter, "The Archaeology of Roman Palestine," in *Near Eastern Archaeology* (Atlanta, GA: Scholars Press for the American Schools of Oriental Research, 2001), 182.

69. Andrea M. Berlin, "The Plain Wares," in *The Hellenistic and Roman Pottery*, ed. Sharon C. Herbert (Ann Arbor: Kelsey Museum of the University of Michigan, 1997), 32.

5

CONCLUSION

The images of Galilee in the first century CE that are often pro-
mulgated in the literature seem to exist without regard to the
archaeological evidence. Although the integration of archaeological
data with these social reconstructions has occurred in the past, those
portraits that have influenced scholarship until recently seem to
selectively choose portions of that evidence and so create portraits
of the Galilee that do not stand up to rigorous comparison with the
information provided by the evidence of contemporary excavations.
Even some contemporary utilizations of archaeological data to sub-
stantiate reconstructions of the life of Jesus and the first century in
the region seem to fall prey to selective use of sources, both literary
and archaeological.[1]

As others have noted, scholars point to a supposed history of the
region that is composed of a series of successive invasions by foreign
powers who both oppress the remaining indigenous population and
infuse it with a mixture of new inhabitants. This is, when checked
against the evidence, a view that cannot be supported. It is, however, a sort of half-truth. As noted in the record at Bethsaida, we
see clearly that the site was ruled successively by a series of foreign
non-Jewish overlords. Beginning with the Assyrian destruction of
Iron Age II, then later perhaps by the Persians, then certainly by the

Ptolemies, the Seleucids, and finally, in terms of the scope of this study, the Romans, Bethsaida was subject to foreign rule. Only for the brief period of the Hasmonean kingdom was the political situation entirely in Jewish hands.

However, while we note the pattern of political rule, we do not see a series of enforced repopulation efforts that are said to have occurred to produce the diverse mixture of inhabitants presupposed by many reconstructions of first century CE Galilee. Instead, the record witnesses to a depopulation following the Assyrian conquest, no repopulation during the Persian period, and then a slow resettlement by a group that seems to be affiliated with the Hellenistic coast.

The material culture that is uncovered seems to reflect a kind of "business as usual" impact of the political upheaval upon the settlement. This is in line with the observation by Dennis Groh that the testimony of material culture is one of "how quickly the average person needs to put life back together again."[2] They seem to continue more or less unimpeded by the changing political climate of the larger region, unlike what occurred at the end of the Iron Age at the site.

While there may be some evidence that the initial repopulation may have been carried out, at least in part, by military veterans, there does not appear to be any evidence of a mandated repopulation by a ruling power sending colonists into the town. The resettlement seems to begin gradually under the Ptolemies and build somewhat more dramatically under the Seleucids. The population consisted of those reflecting the dominant Hellenistic culture of the coast, presumably therefore pagan. Sean Freyne has suggested that paying particular attention to this transition phase between Ptolemaic and Seleucid administration of control is crucial to understanding the Hellenization of the Galilee. The question of the religious preference of a settlement, however, does not seem to be based on the systematic implementation of a "pan-Greek culture" but rather local attachment to a particular deity or deities.[3]

It was only during the Hasmonean takeover of the site that we see a sudden dramatic shifting in the apparent ethnic composition of the population. But whether as a direct result of enforcement of Aristobulus I's decree mandating the conversion of the inhabitants[4]—or their emigration—or as the result of replacement of the populace by new settlers from the Jewish south, cannot be completely determined by this study. However, since there is such a dramatic shift in the material culture of the settlement, it is clear that Bethsaida had a largely Jewish population in the early first century CE. In any event, therefore, those that dwelt in the site were, at least for a preceding few generations, "behaving Jewishly," to use Marianne Sawicki's term:

> To "behave Jewishly" in colonized Roman Galilee must have had something to do with maintaining identity while moving through a built environment designed to gobble up indigenous culture, wealth, and labor into the imperial maw of worldwide trade.[5]

Thus, the portrait from Bethsaida indicates that there was no eclectic mix of Greek and Jew, pagan and monotheist in this part of the Galilee in the first century CE. This is made all the more apparent when one compares Bethsaida to a recognized pagan site such as any of the Decapolis cities. If there are pagans at Bethsaida during the first century CE, they are largely invisible in the archaeological record. This is in direct contrast to the second or early first centuries BCE. Pagan figurines, ceramic styles, and even coinage, which were in great abundance during that earlier time, suddenly fail to appear.

This detailed analysis shows that the Bethsaida evidence presented fits comfortably within and makes a significant contribution to the archaeological discussion of the first century CE in the Galilee region.

The importance of having recovered data from secure archaeological contexts can hardly be overstated. The material recovered from Bethsaida derives from a well-preserved, primary archaeological context, which has had only limited disturbance from human activity subsequent to the period under investigation. This enables one to be able to draw substantial evidence for a new general understanding of the material culture and history of the region.

This new understanding seems propitious and particularly important in view of the current debate over the interpretation of archaeological data that scholars have currently associated with the first century CE. Though a substantial number of excavated sites have attested first century CE strata, the precise stratigraphy and related absolute dates have often been confused by interpreters. The result has been to muddle the ethnic and religious affiliations of the associated population groups. Despite the existence of several well-known New Testament sites, such as Nazareth or Capernaum, the understanding of the first century has lagged because of a scarcity of close examination of the archaeological evidence as well as its selective use mainly to support hypotheses developed from the literary corpus. Hopefully, the Bethsaida evidence can now be utilized to help evaluate remains from other contexts as well.

The evidence from Bethsaida itself has implications for the sociopolitical development of the region in this period. In view of the well-established archaeological chronology of settlement patterns at the site, the shift in the cultural affiliation of the varying archaeological stratigraphical contexts between the non-Jewish coast with its Hellenistic empires to the Jewish Galilee and the Jewish Judean culture is clear. We may therefore reasonably associate Bethsaida with a Jewish Galilee and call into question any reconstruction of the area that overstates a Gentile or non-Jewish presence among the population there. The discussion of a "Galilee of the Gentiles" in biblical scholarship and the particularity of its culture seems in light of this to unreasonably emphasize a large gentile presence in the first century CE. The distinctive characteristic of Bethsaida, and its wider context of Galilee, was a high degree of Jewish cultural autonomy.

However, this cultural setting changed again in the second century CE when Roman troops arrived in the region for a long-term stay bringing with them support personnel and families. This "occupation" represents a significant change compared to the prior short-term forays into the region during times of unrest. Beginning at about 120 CE,[6] there is evidence for the increasing influence of gentiles in the region. This new presence can be seen in the actions at Sepphoris and Tiberias where coins take on more pagan imagery and Sepphoris changes its name to Diocaesarea. This may account as well for the renewed presence of "pagan" artifacts and ceramic typologies at Bethsaida, as elsewhere in Jewish Galilee. The return of these items is noted in the Bethsaida corpus from the second century CE until its abandonment sometime in the early fourth century.

HOW JEWISH? HOW HELLENISTIC?

While a complete discussion of how extensively the enculturation of Hellenism penetrated into Galilee is beyond the evidence we are examining from Bethsaida alone, we can make a few observations about how deeply the Greco-Roman world had penetrated and interlaced with the Galilean context for our Bethsaida perspective. One observation is that despite the change from a coastal oriented pagan presence in the Hellenistic period to a Jewish oriented society at Bethsaida in the first century BCE/CE, there was not a complete break with Hellenistic culture. That can be seen even in the "conspicuous consumption" exhibited in the use of ceramic vessels that differed by their lack of pagan decoration from their non-Jewish counterparts and possible models. Andrea Berlin notes that "the archaeological evidence shows that Jews throughout Judea, Galilee and Gaulinitis were closely linked by religious practices."[7] This religious attitude manifested itself in activities that were incorporated in their daily lives that changed the material culture: "They began using stone vessels and a specific new form of oil lamp to further distinguish and identify themselves."[8] The basic typology of other ceramics was still consistent with the Hellenistic corpus though lacking the decorative motifs. So while the dominant culture may have been Jewish, the larger Hellenistic cultural context still has influence. No one has yet found in the region a village entirely unaffected by Hellenistic goods and materials.

What were the possible sources of this continued interaction and influence? It should be noted that the Hasmonean and Herodian settlers would have come from areas equally influenced by Greek culture. The Jerusalem headquarters of those settlers had already experienced a degree of Hellenization under the reign of the Hellenistic empires of Alexander, the Ptolemies, and the Seleucids. In fact, Herod and the subsequent Herodian dynasty were primary advocates of Greco-Roman urbanization of the various kingdoms they ruled. This does not mean we should have expected the "Athens-on-the-Kinneret" mentioned in the introduction, but it does mean that the presence of Greeks, Romans, or other Hellenized population groups outside of the Jewish ethnic group would not necessarily need to be present in the area for Hellenization to have continued to occur.

It is important to remember, however, that the shift in material culture following the Hasmonean expansion to Bethsaida does clearly indicate that the lack of the presence of those "foreign" groups meant that Hellenization may have occurred at a different "rate" or have taken a different form than when those groups were present in the earlier periods. In addition, it is likely that Hellenization took a much different form again after the arrival of the long term presence of Roman troops in the second century CE.

What we can say too from the record at Bethsaida is that the architectural and city plan at Bethsaida does not warrant claiming that a tide of Hellenism had washed over the region erasing any and all local traditions. This might have occurred had Bethsaida survived and thrived during the post-revolt period and become more like some other cities in the Galilee, such as in Sepphoris and Tiberias, as they remodeled and expanded in the later fourth century CE to become more classically Hellenistic cities. But such is not the case in the material record at first century CE Bethsaida. The record is also unlike the pattern we see in the Decapolis cities that were founded contemporaneously with Bethsaida.

Thus, during the *first century CE*, while not isolated from the larger Greco-Roman cultural trends, Bethsaida manifests an interplay between local culture and Greco-Roman culture in a way that the dominant role of the local culture (i.e., Jewish) is seen. This interplay would look very different either before or after this relatively brief interlude.

That observation highlights the importance for any social reconstruction of the first century CE in Galilee of avoiding extrapolation in any direction toward the first century CE. That is, third, second and early first century BCE Bethsaida/Galilee should not be used to understand first century CE Bethsaida. The population present at Bethsaida significantly changed in the late first century BCE and early first century CE. Likewise, mid-second to fourth century CE Bethsaida/Galilee should not be used to demonstrate the nature of the social interaction between Jew and pagan in the first century CE. This view to some extent argues against Dennis Groh's position that one should learn to read the first century CE backward from the fourth century CE and to not think of the first century CE as "canonical time" matching the canonical documents.[9] While there is no intention to create a "special age" for the first century CE, I hope that this book has demonstrated the peculiar matrix of the first century CE at Bethsaida while not ignoring the previous influences. The prior and later data are almost irrelevant for the rather unique setting of the first century CE because the population mix and relative numbers of differing ethnic groups seems to have significantly changed. Thus, scholarly social reconstructions that ignore the predominately Jewish character of Bethsaida and its environs are likely to distort the first century CE context as observed in the material record.

Having stated the conclusions forcefully, now it is time to state the constraints that preclude absolute certainty for these statements. The task has been to explore the relation between Bethsaida and its Galilean context and the relationship between the archaeological record and reconstructions by social historians and other scholars. Were there any gentiles at Bethsaida? We have not spoken to the precise ratio of population Jewish to gentile. We have not addressed class dimensions of the society at Bethsaida and whether or not issues of class distinction may have accounted for some of the transition of material culture witnessed. The issue is ultimately unanswerable solely from the material record since it requires a precision regarding relative proportion and influence that is not attainable from the present evidence. However, the evidence does not support a portrayal of Jesus, or anyone else, living amidst the gentiles of Galilee but scrupulously avoiding contact with them. That is, in the material record from Bethsaida, one cannot find support for reconstructing a settlement dominated by a gentile population of any significance in the first century CE.

Although the area of the tell that produced the remains examined in this book remains only a small portion of the site, the overall size of the settlement exposed thus far indicates that this was more than an isolated fishing village. It was at least the size of a significant town and therefore should exhibit the normal urban characteristic of the control over both natural and human resources exhibited in this region. Thus, what is determined from the site may be expected to be true to some significant degree in its related hinterland.

In any event, the appearance of the significant Jewish ethnic markers in what was a substantial settlement at the edge of the Jewish Galilee in the first century CE demonstrates a movement toward at least selective detachment from the dominant Hellenistic culture. As reflected in the literary corpus, the search for the best expression of correct living may be witnessed in the selective appropriation of the larger cultural material available. In the basic issues of daily life an implicit commentary on values and alternative social realities is glimpsed. These suggest ways that are often at odds with those asserted by priests, rabbis, and overlords. The ambiguity between literarily expressed ideals and variation in the application of them may provide our best tool for understanding the existing social world.

Yet, the intrusion of the Hellenistic world into the arena of Galilee cannot be minimized. It would seem, however, that while the Empire, whether Hellenistic or Roman, would not tolerate independent political operations that could have interfered with its long-term exploitation of the region, either it did not desire an exclusive religious or social position or it could not ultimately limit local opinion and practice, so that a form of pluralism existed within the local society, as in the international community.

Modern sociology uses the term "acculturalization" to describe the phenomena that result when groups from different cultures come into continuous first-hand contact. The process results in changes to either or both of the original cultural groups.[10] Elayi and Sapin suggest a less direct mode of interaction that may or may not produce this kind of cultural mutation. In fact, their term of "interculturality" allows for more forms of exchange and more leeway in its results.[11] They develop this idea to frame their questions about, for example, Phoenician use of Greek ritual objects: "We must decide whether their usage implied a radical modification of these rituals, or whether they were treated simply as interchangeable instruments."[12] In our case, however, we have the converse phenomenon. We have in evidence a radical nonusage of ritual objects and an implied radical rejection of the accompanying ritual. It would seem therefore that we might be able to state with some high probability that the nonusage of some items and motifs, or the local modification of common non-Jewish items to an accepted and locally used form, would indicate that items were not innocently appropriated for aesthetic reasons, nor was there a morphological equivalency created between objects. This kind of "interculturality" indicates a resistance to the Roman-Hellenistic societal matrix and shows that there were constraining forces on the degree to which Jewish society was Hellenized in the first century CE.

However, as Douglas Edwards regarding discussing the first century CE in the Galilee states, "The Galilee in the first two centuries of this era was no 'Semitic enclave surrounded by Hellenism,' as M. Goodman has phrased it."[13] The interaction of influences, both Semitic and Hellenic, created the cultural matrix of evidence in first century Bethsaida that lies between that of isolation and assimilation.

These forces to some degree may have found their origins in the development of the region during the prior centuries. If our reconstructed chronology of settlement in the region is correct, then the population of Bethsaida in the late first century BCE consisted mainly of Judean colonists moving northward during the Hasmonean expansion. This movement of population was a part of the economic, political, and cultural impact of the Hellenistic and Roman empires. This may mean that one should reexamine theories that consider the population as converted remnants of semi-pagan Iron

Age Israelite and colonial Phoenicians and Seleucids. All groups, Jewish and non-Jewish, were agrarian communities dominated by Hellenistic developments accelerated by Roman society.

Bethsaida was Jewish Bethsaida in Roman Palestine in the first century CE.

NOTES

1. Much has been made of the process of urbanization and its impact on Roman Galilee and the nascent Jesus movement. See, for example, Richard A. Batey, *Jesus and the Forgotten City: New Light on Sepphoris and the Urban World of Jesus* (Grand Rapids, MI: Baker Book House, 1991), Frederick M. Strickert, *Bethsaida: Home of the Apostles* (Collegeville, MN: Liturgical Press, 1998) or Leif E. Vaage, *Galilean Upstarts: Jesus' First Followers According to Q* (Valley Forge, PA: Trinity Press International, 1994). Andrew Overman correctly points out that many of these newer reconstructions are dependent upon support or contradiction of the "Peasant-Jesus paradigm" and are still primarily based on a literary reading of Josephus that seeks "some apprehendable, contemporary reconstruction of the Jesus of history." Andrew J. Overman, "Jesus of Galilee and the Historical Present," in *Archaeology and the Galilee: Texts and Contexts in the Graeco-Roman and Byzantine Periods* (Atlanta, GA: Scholars Press, 1997), 72.

2. Dennis E. Groh, "The Clash Between Literary and Archaeological Models," in *Archaeology and the Galilee Texts and Contexts in the Graeco-Roman and Byzantine Periods* (Atlanta, GA: Scholars Press, 1997), 30.

3. Sean Freyne, "Galilean Studies: Old Issues and New Questions," in *Religion, Ethnicity, and Identity in Ancient Galilee*, ed. Jürgen Zangenberg, Harold W. Attridge, and Dale B. Martin, Wissenschaftliche Untersuchungen Zum Neuen Testament (Tübingen: Mohr Siebeck, 2007), 19.

4. Antiquities 13.318–319.

5. Marianne Sawicki, "Spatial Management of Gender and Labor," in *Archaeology and the Galilee: Texts and Contexts in the Graeco-Roman and Byzantine Periods* (Atlanta, GA: Scholars Press, 1997), 9.

6. Zeev Safrai, "The Roman Army in the Galilee," in *The Galilee in Late Antiquity*, ed. Lee I. Levine (New York and Cambridge, MA: Jewish Theological Seminary of America Distributed by Harvard University Press,

1992), 104f. Safrai notes the start of the occupation of the Galilee by a Roman legion.

7. Berlin, *Jewish Life Before the Revolt: The Archaeological Evidence*, 2.

8. Berlin, *Jewish Life Before the Revolt: The Archaeological Evidence*, 2.

9. Groh, "The Clash Between Literary and Archaeological Models," 32.

10. R. Redfield, R. Linton, and M. J. Herskovits, "Memorandum for the Study of Acculturation," in *American Anthropologist* (Washington, DC: American Anthropological Association, 1936).

11. Elayi and Sapin, *Beyond the River: New Perspectives on Transeuphratene*, 140–41.

12. Elayi and Sapin, *Beyond the River: New Perspectives on Transeuphratene*, 142–43.

13. Douglas R. Edwards, "The Socio-Economic and Cultural Ethos of the Lower Galilee in the First Century: Implications for the Nascent Jesus Movement," in *The Galilee in Late Antiquity*, ed. Lee I. Levine (New York and Cambridge, MA: Jewish Theological Seminary of America Distributed by Harvard University Press, 1992), 68.

EXCURSUS 1

The "Temple" of Bethsaida

Recent work conducted by the author in the area surrounding the enigmatic building located in squares G-K 51–53 in Stratum 2 adds to the understanding of the structure. Particular attention is given to the dating of construction and use(s) that may have been made of the structure. Understanding the purpose of this building may provide a better understanding of the societal make-up and religious orientation of late second Temple period Bethsaida.

REVISITING THE TEMPLE OF BETHSAIDA[1]

We are all aware of that fact that the data we employ in our reconstructions of the past is subject to interpretation. How data is framed is important as to how data is understood. In archaeological excavation, we deal with the fragmentary remnants of human activity in the forms of artifacts and architectural features. When working from the material culture we begin in fieldwork by treating the data as something that is at first only something to record and to think about later when considering the choices, details, and life pathways of the people and culture we wish to know better. However, one does not approach a site such as Bethsaida completely divorced from a framework of expectations from literary sources. Unfortunately, these literary sources and their history of interpretation can sometimes unduly bias field research interpretations. At Bethsaida this unfortunately may have been often a recurring pitfall. In particular, scholars often approach Bethsaida with a portrait of an early Jewish fishing village complete with synagogue. A recent article in *Studia Judaica* by Przemyslaw Nowogórski illustrates this fact.[2] In the article, Nowogórski reiterates an often found presumption, one in which a presumed culture of Judaism in the first century requires a synagogal structure complete with prayer hall, store room, miqvah, bet din, courtyard, and school. The "Bethsaida of Jesus" must be Jewish in this reconstructed Talmudic fashion.

The actual archaeological data for the public structure referred to in the article indicates that this type of reconstruction is far too fanciful.

First uncovered in 1988, but only later fully recognized as a public structure of importance, the "temple" of Bethsaida has variously been called by the excavators a synagogue, a pagan temple, and more specifically a temple of the imperial cult. A fairly exhaustive treatment of the early findings was published in 1998. In that article the reasons were given for identifying the structure as a temple.[3]

The structure under question was originally interpreted as a temple with distyle in antis. Most of the identifying characteristics have to do with the architecture as interpreted from the remnants of the walls of the building. The presumed cella is fairly intact, but other components are less well preserved due to a Syrian military trench that cut across the eastern portions of the building and other earlier looting of materials in antiquity. The structure is a rectangle of roughly 6 × 20 meters facing very slightly south of east—that is, perhaps oriented toward the sunrise. The dimensions of the structure actually closely approach the ratio of the golden rectangles thought by some to be important to temple construction. The cella approximates 6.8 × 10.9 meters. The pronaos, which because of modern disturbance is in very poor preservation, is likewise close to an appropriate dimension approximately 6.8 × 5 meters. So while the structure is somewhat diminutive, it is classically designed to some extent.

Two columns portions were found associated with the building. One was found *in situ* on a base in a location where the antis to the east would have been. The other was found displaced, tumbled in the cella. There are many artifacts associated with the building in earlier reports, but none of these were found *in* the building itself but to the west and southeast. These finds include the bronze incense shovel,[4] a figurine of a woman with Roman style hair and veil that is identified as Livia Julia,[5] pits filled with intact vessels, such as jugs, that may have been used in a cultic practice, and most recently nested bronze bowls and "pregnant lady" figurines.[6]

No podium has been detected. However, a sort of temenos may have existed in the form of a plastered plaza. Indications of this have been uncovered in recent seasons.[7] A plastered floor surface has been detected on the southern wall extending some 5 meters at least to the south.

In sum, as of 2006, the researchers, while admitting the limitations of parallel with traditional Hellenistic temple architecture, suggest that this obviously public structure may best be interpreted as such.

Certainly the dimensions and features are more like this Hellenistic form of structure than any of the proposed models for early synagogal architecture. The candidate structures, such as the synagogue of Gamla, Masada, Migdal, and Herodian, are more squarish and present more open space in the major room. For example, the Gamla structure is 25.5 × 17 m, Masada 15 × 12 m, Herodium 15.15 × 10.6 m.[8]

STRATIGRAPHY

Part of the context of any structure on an archaeological site includes not just its x-y spatial orientation and relationship to other structures, but also its temporal location. At Bethsaida, stratum 2 is designated as the Hellenistic–Early Roman stratum. However, as work has progressed in recent years, this designation needs to be further developed. The author has now constructed a more nuanced understanding of occupation levels during this period that necessitates a further refining of the stratigraphy.

I wish to illustrate this with reference to key material indicators that we have found at Bethsaida: coins, stamped amphora handles, glassware, ceramics, stoneware, and architectural remains. Of course, all of these indicators taken singularly are not as compelling as seeing them in an interrelated whole.[9]

Bethsaida was destroyed sometime during the Iron Age II ostensibly during the Assyrian conquest of the region in the late eighth century. There is clear evidence of massive destruction at the huge Iron Age city-gate as well as little evidence of occupation for nearly five centuries following that catastrophic event. There have been only very fragmentary finds from the Iron Age III and Persian periods and no evidence of construction during these times.

What we see instead is a sudden period of construction and re-occupation beginning during the Hellenistic period in the third century BCE. I suggest that based upon the coin evidence this may well have occurred during the reign of Ptolemy II, perhaps prior to the First Syrian War (274–271 BCE). However, control seems to pass to the Seleucids under Antiochus III some time following the fourth Syrian War (217 BCE), perhaps as late as 200 BCE. Subsequent to this we find no later Ptolemaic coins. There is no evidence of destruction at the site, merely a change in coinage that would indicate a change of governmental orientation. Seleucid control appears to be maintained until John Hyrcanus I's expansion into the Golan area in the late second century BCE. Again, control seems to be "peaceably" transferred. Likewise we see evidence of a transition to Herodian control as part of Herod's assuming the throne.

Therefore, I suggest that Stratum 2 may be subdivided into at least 4 distinct periods:[10] Stratum 2A is Ptolemaic period—perhaps prior to the First Syrian War (274–271 BCE); Stratum 2B is Seleucid, as control seems to pass to the Seleucids under Antiochus III some time following the fourth Syrian War (217 BCE) perhaps as late as 200 BCE; Stratum 2C is Hasmonean/Herodian, reflecting John Hyrcanus I's expansion into the Golan area in the late second century BCE; and Stratum 2D is Later Roman. The material culture of the site changes substantially during the transition from Seleucid to Jewish control, and the material culture can be used to distinguish levels by content, if by no other means (i.e., the difference in stratigraphy).[11] The pottery at Bethsaida shows a clear change from a coastal import oriented ware to a more local variety in the first centuries BCE/CE. So it should be possible to clearly distinguish stratum 2 in two segments—2AB and 2C.

Of importance for the "temple" building, this subdivided stratigraphy would allow a closer approximation of the construction date. From my latest work, I propose that the original building construction is likely to have taken place during the 2AB period, the one in which the prosperity and size of the population would be likely to have enabled such public building programs. One may perhaps cautiously refine this further to the Stratum 2A since Ptolemaic coins and Phoenician figurines have been found in the layers that are associated with construction in the area just south of the temple.

In any case, the "temple" area buildings appear to have been constructed *prior* to Stratum 2C. The temple building itself seems to reside on the same level as the flagstone pavement that extends to the south and that has been dated to the Hellenistic period by ceramic and coin data.

On top of this pavement several walls were later constructed. One of those walls was W 904, a one meter width wall of two faces of stretcher/header design with regular size stones. This wall design is typical of the better Hellenistic architecture at Bethsaida. Coin data from the locus has not been finally analyzed, but the ceramics are indicative of the second century BCE. Thus, a construction date relative to this wall which is of similar construction technique to those found in the temple seems to fit in time frame of the earliest layer at the site—Stratum 2A Ptolemaic—and certainly before the change to the less prosperous Hasmonean orientation.

While this does not resolve the purpose of the building under discussion, it does make less likely any identification of the building *in its initial usage* and construction as a synagogue or even "proto-synagogue." This does not preclude a later appropriation of the building for that use or other purposes.

There is considerable re-organization of the entire area during the later phases of the period under investigation. The structure of the building was modified and the western antis removed at some later point to reach a large circular structure, likely a storage pit whose construction may have predated the Hellenistic occupation of the site, that was located to the west of the building. Thus, it is possible to imagine that even if it were a temple at some point there may have been a significant change in the building's use.

OTHER INDICATIVES

In the Stratum 2C layer approximately ten meters south of the building, fragments of three limestone vessels have been found along with local Galilean ceramics and Herodian lamp fragments.[12] These, as discussed previously in the main text, are taken as indicative of Jewish presence. In Stratum 2A/B, figurines were found that are clearly of Hellenistic origin, and the ceramic collection was of the more typically Hellenistic pattern found at Bethsaida during that period.[13]

Early researchers pointed to other figurine fragments and a bronze incense shovel as evidence for deigning the building a temple. However, the stratigraphy was not carefully examined to detect the subdivision in Stratum 2.[14]

The recently completed analysis of faunal remains by Dr. Toni Fisher points to an interesting conclusion about the building. Dr. Fisher notes that the building yielded a high number of cattle bones in a ratio to caprids that is well above that of other Hellenistic Roman loci at the site.[15] This leads to speculation that the building served a function among the elite of the site. Also notable is the fact that cattle are the preferred sacrificial animal in many pagan temple cults.

Unfortunately, once again, the stratigraphy of the bones has so far been collapsed into a stratum covering the whole of the Hellenistic/ Roman period.

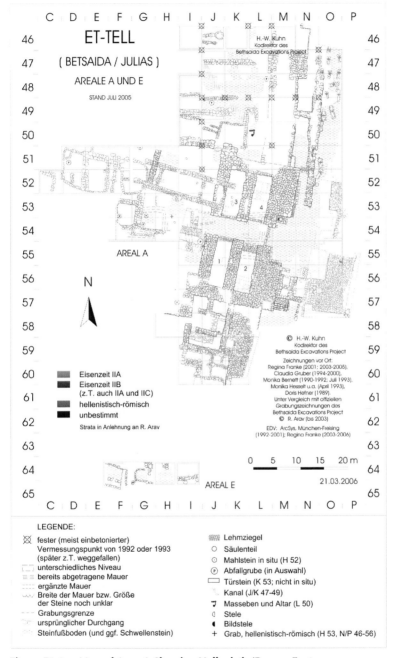

Figure E1.1. Map of Area A Showing Hellenistic/Roman Features
Source: Professor emeritus Dr. Heinz-Wolfgang Kuhn, Ludwig-Maximilians-Universität München

Figure E1.2. Map of "Temple" and Immediate Context
Source: Dr. Rami Arav, Bethsaida Director of Excavations, University of Nebraska at Omaha

CONCLUSION

In this revisit to the temple of Bethsaida, only very limited pro-nouncements about the structure may truly be substantiated. The building is likely to have been constructed during the second century BCE. This somewhat limits the interpretations that may be placed upon the structure. It was not likely to have been constructed as either a proto-synagogue or an imperial cult temple. Both of those suggestions presuppose a construction date other than seems plausible. A possibility, if it were truly a pagan temple as suggested

Figure E1.3.   Aerial Photo of Area A Showing "Temple" Building
Source: Paul Bauman, Principal Geophysicist, WorleyParsons Komex

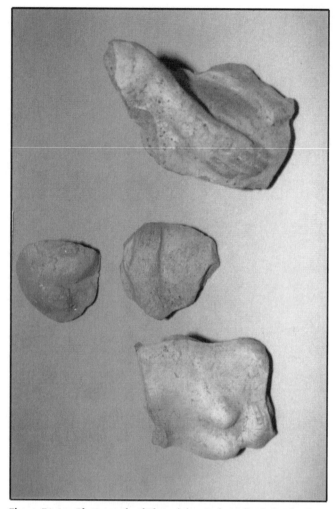

Figure E1.4.   Photograph of Phoenician Style Hellenistic Figurines
Source: Hanan Shafir, Ramat Hasharon, Israel, Bethsaida Staff Photographer 2006–present

by its form and construction, is that it may have been a local cultic installation created during the Seleucid control period and perhaps some sort of temple related to fertility—but that is speculation based on the presence of female figurines of pregnant women that parallel findings from the Phoenician coast.[16]

Nonetheless, since there is a lack of household ceramics, or, for that matter, much of any kind of ceramic evidence within the struc-

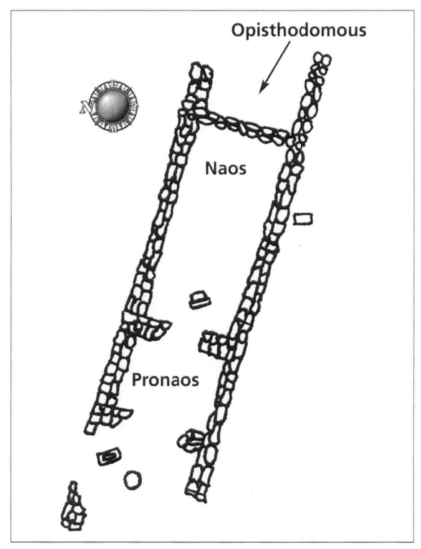

Figure E1.5. Diagram of Suggested Temple Plan
Source: Dr. Fred Strickert, Professor of Religion, Wartburg College

ture itself, it would seem to support the tentative conclusion that the building is indeed a public structure.

It is still possible, however, that in its later phases, the building could have been renovated or patterned into either a proto-synagogue or an imperial cult site. However, it is also possible that it was used for an entirely different purpose, however unknown at the present.

NOTES

1. An earlier version of this excursus was first presented as a conference paper: Carl Savage, "Revisiting the Temple at Bethsaida," Society for Biblical Literature (Philadelphia, 2006).

2. Przemyslaw Nowogórski, "Protosynagoga W Betsaidzie: Hipotetyczna Interpretacja Budynku Na Area A Na Et-Tell (Betsaida)," in *Studia Judaica Biuletyn Polskiego Towarzystwa Studiów Zydowskich* (Kraków: Ksiegarnia Akademicka, 2004), 41–47. In the article the author makes a case for Bethsaida's public building in Area A being a proto-synagogue based largely on the conjecture that since Bethsaida was Jewish, it must have had a synagogue.

3. The building was superimposed over the Iron Age city gate chamber 3 and was disturbed by a Syrian military trench as well as a Syrian military position that was built on top of what could have been the *pronaos*. Arav lists the general ground plan, the stone decorations, and the small finds found in the vicinity of the building as reasons for identifying the building as a temple. The main room of the building was found to be "totally empty." Rami Arav, "Bethsaida Excavations: Preliminary Report, 1994–1996," in *The Bethsaida Excavations Project Reports & Contextual Studies*, ed. Rami Arav (Kirksville, MO: Thomas Jefferson University Press, 1999), 18–24.

4. Richard A. Freund, "The Incense Shovel of Bethsaida and Synagogue Iconography in Late Antiquity," in *The Bethsaida Excavations Project Reports & Contextual Studies*, ed. Rami Arav (Kirksville, MO: Thomas Jefferson University Press, 1999), 413–59. The incense shovel was discovered in a pit 10 meters southwest of the building.

5. Measuring 2 cm by 4 cm this mold made head of a woman was identified as Livia Julia in the role of Augustan priestess by Arav in 1995. Rami Arav, "Bethsaida Excavations: Preliminary Report, 1987–1993," in *The Bethsaida Excavations Project Reports & Contextual Studies*, ed. Rami Arav (Kirksville, MO: Thomas Jefferson University Press, 1995), 21.

6. The first two items were published previously. The remaining items are as yet unpublished. The pit with vessels was uncovered in 1999 and fully excavated in 2001. The bronze bowls were discovered in 2006. The

figurines were found in 2005, 2006, and 2007. All were found in the vicinity of the temple building but not within its confines.

7. See figure E1.3. The area south of the "temple" contains a pavement of fairly large cobblestones as is apparent in the photograph of the area. Above the cobbles was an extensive plastered surface of nearly 8 cm thickness in places.

8. For an overview on these synagogues see Donald D. Binder, *Into the Temple Courts the Place of the Synagogues in the Second Temple Period* (Atlanta, GA: Society of Biblical Literature, 1999), 162ff. For more on Herodium, see Doron Chen, "The Design of the Ancient Synagogues in Judea: Masada and Herodium," in *Bulletin of the American Schools of Oriental Research* (Missoula, MT: Scholars Press, 1980), 37–40 or Gideon Foester, "The Synagogues at Masada and Herodium," in *Ancient Synagogues Revealed*, ed. Lee I. Levine (Jerusalem: Israel Exploration Society, 1982), 24–29. For more on Gamla, see Shmaryahu Gutmann, "Gamala," in *The New Encyclopedia of Archaeological Excavations in the Holy Land*, ed. Ephraim Stern (Jerusalem New York: Israel Exploration Society and Carta Simon and Schuster, 1993), 460–61.

9. The brief summary in the following two paragraphs was covered in much greater detail in the body of chapter 4.

10. Arav originally stated that occupation Level 2 consisted of "Four phases of occupation between the Early Hellenistic period and the Early Roman period (333 BCE–67 CE)" but does not give any elaboration of how this was derived. Arav, "Bethsaida Excavations: Preliminary Report, 1987–1993," 6. In the report containing this definition there is no further mention of the four phases when discussing the finds. In the report for 1994–1996, he discusses the difficulty in distinguishing the "layers" in this level because of the method of construction involving the reuse of earlier architectural features. He especially notes that "in areas where the hard and durable basalt stones served as the main material of construction, this method was even more intensified." Arav, "Bethsaida Excavations: Preliminary Report, 1994–1996," 18.

11. Normally one would rely on other means to carefully distinguish occupation levels. Traditionally, color, texture, compaction, particle size, and contents and condition of the material being excavated are used as indicators of a transition in usage of an area. Preferably, one will encounter a layer that clearly seals the material from upper layers, such as a floor, but this is not always the case. One would expect to confirm a designation

in one part of the site with that from other loci at the site, thus confirming less secure analyses with better secured ones.

12. These items are discussed in chapter 4.

13. See figure E1.4. These figurines are typical of those found at Tel Dor on the Phoenician coast. See Ephraim Stern, "A Favissa of a Phoenician Sanctuary from Tel Dor," in *The Journal of Jewish Studies* (Cambridge, England, 1982), 35–54. Plate II 4 and 4a on page 52 show the closest parallel to the Bethsaida figurines. This figurine can also be seen in Mazar, *Archaeology of the Land of the Bible: 10,000–586 B.C.E.*, 540.

14. It would be interesting if it proves possible to more carefully determine to which half of Stratum 2 the incense shovel now belongs.

15. Toni Fisher, "This Close to Publishing My Dissertation: Bones Update," Batchelder Biblical Archaeological Conference (Omaha, NE: 2002).

16. Mazar, *Archaeology of the Land of the Bible: 10,000–586 B.C.E.*, 540.

EXCURSUS 2
Identifying Et-Tell
with Bethsaida

SITE LOCATION

The site of Et-Tell/Bethsaida is located on the northeastern corner of the Sea of Galilee on the northern edge of an alluvial plain known as the Beteiha plain and at the southern edge of the Golan Heights plateau lava flow. The roughly oval shaped mound is one of the largest archaeological sites near the Sea of Galilee extending 400 meters long by 200 meters wide, or approximately 20 acres. The highest point of the tell is 165.91 meters below sea level but is nearly 30 meters above the average height of its surrounding terrain (196 meters below sea level) and approximately 45 meters above the present day mean level of the Sea of Galilee. The relative height of the mound gives a commanding view of the entire lake on a clear day.

Access to the site is easiest from the north where the descending Golan plateau reaches to the mound. The eastern slope, where the Iron Age gate and entrance was located, descends sharply to a ravine separating the mound from a small natural hill. Toward the south and west, the mound slopes less steeply toward the Beteiha plain.

The Jordan River runs less than 250 meters west of the mound but two closer water sources provided the settlement with fresh water.

The two springs are located just adjacent to the mound, a small spring to the southeast and a larger one to the southwest.

THE LOST CITY

The direct literary evidence for Bethsaida appears to cease in the third century CE, about the same time that the archaeological record also becomes discontinuous. Yet the interest in its location remained high because Bethsaida is mentioned seven times in the New Testament gospels. Early pilgrim literature frequently mentions visits to the site of Bethsaida, but their accounts are vague and often contradictory.[1]

In the nineteenth century, initial surveys of the Holy Land sought to identify as many places as possible that were mentioned in the Bible with sites in Palestine. The search was conducted most effectively by Edward Robinson. In 1838 he visited a mound simply known as Et-Tell (the mound), located on the northeast corner of the alluvial plain known as the Beteiha Plain. Although the mound stood nearly one and a half miles from the lakeshore, Robinson identified it as Bethsaida.

Later in the 1870s Gotlieb Schumacher questioned this designation precisely because Et-Tell was so distant from the water. In his mind, Et-Tell could not possibly be equated with the fishing community, Bethsaida, based upon the description of Bethsaida's location in the gospel literature. He proposed that a ruin closer to the lake by the name of el-Araj was the more likely candidate for biblical Bethsaida.

The debate continued, with some scholars supporting Robinson's position and others Schumacher's, and a third group suggesting that there were in fact two Bethsaidas: the fishing village el-Araj, and the city that Philip named Julias, Et-Tell.

GEOLOGICAL CONSIDERATIONS FOR IDENTIFICATION

Schumacher was correct in his assessment of Et-Tell's location in comparison to the New Testament description of the location of Bethsaida; the present day geography does not match the first century account. Present day el-Araj, on the other hand, does more closely match the first century description. However, as Jack Shroder and Moshe Inbar point out, "People are generally unsophisticated about long-term geologic change common to areas with active tectonism, delta-growth, and changing water levels, so that a site that is no longer on the coast would not be recognized as a former port."[2] Thus, as a result, el-Araj has received attention as the potential site of Bethsaida.

Shroder and Inbar dismiss el-Araj on geologic grounds because its location would make it subject to periodic seasonal flooding and occasional catastrophic inundation from seismic tsunami waves.[3] Because of the geological instability and its low lying position on the alluvial plain, el-Araj is relegated as an unsuitable "malarial site, subject to seasonal lake floods, tsunami waves and Jordan River flood inundation" by Shroder and Inbar.[4]

The problem remains, however, to determine the first century CE geography for the mound of Et-Tell. Specifically, could its location have matched that found in the early sources?

Shroder and Inbar demonstrate that the Beteiha plain coastline of the Et-Tell site had shifted from a lagoonal environment with easy access to the main body of the lake to the present day dry-land environment through a combination of three mechanisms. The shift occurred through a "combination of uplift of the land along the Dead Sea–Jordan rift or transform fault system ('shore-up' hypothesis), change of water level in the unstable Sea of Galilee ('water-down' hypothesis), and building out of the shoreline in the Jordan delta past Bethsaida ('shore-out' hypothesis.)"[5] In a subsequent article Shroder et al. determined that there was indeed evidence that "quiet water" was to be found at the base of the Et-Tell site at approximately the turn of the eras. Thus the site was capable of supporting industry dependent on navigable contact with the lake.[6]

ARCHAEOLOGICAL EVIDENCE

The material culture evidence for site identification has been presented for Et-Tell in the body of this present work. As always, however, when dealing with the issue of site identification without *in situ* epigraphical evidence in the form of inscriptions on architecture or recovered documentary material, one cannot present a conclusive case. Nonetheless, one can say with certainty that none of the other contenders for the site designation of Bethsaida present a plausible ceramic, numismatic, or architectural argument. El-Araj, for example, has been shown to be a one level occupational site from the Byzantine era built upon beach sediments. Ground penetration radar survey of the site was conducted and revealed only beach sedimentation below a single layer occupation level.[7] While some have claimed to have found first-century pottery and coins below the surface at el-Araj, these were found in sand and not in an architectural context.[8] The pottery associated with the visible surface occupation level dates to the Byzantine period only.[9] Thus Et-Tell is the only viable alternative for identification as the first-century settlement of Bethsaida.

NOTES

1. Elizabeth McNamer, "Medieval Pilgrim Accounts of Bethsaida and the Bethsaida Controversy," in *The Bethsaida Excavations Project Reports & Contextual Studies*, ed. Rami Arav (Kirksville, MO: Thomas Jefferson University Press, 1999), 397–412.

2. Jack F. Shroder and Moshe Inbar, "Geologic and Geographic Background to the Bethsaida Excavations," in *The Bethsaida Excavations Project Reports & Contextual Studies*, ed. Rami Arav (Kirksville, MO: Thomas Jefferson University Press, 1995), 65.

3. Shroder and Inbar's extensive article details both the record of seismic activity and the record of tsunami waves. Shroder and Inbar, "Geologic and Geographic Background to the Bethsaida Excavations," 67–76.

4. Shroder and Inbar, "Geologic and Geographic Background to the Bethsaida Excavations," 76.

5. Jack F. Shroder, Michael Bishop, Kevin J. Cornwell, and Moshe Inbar, "Catastrophic Geomorphic Processes and Bethsaida Archaeology, Israel," in *The Bethsaida Excavations Project Reports & Contextual Studies*, ed. Rami Arav (Kirksville, MO: Thomas Jefferson University Press, 1999), 115–73.

6. Shroder, Bishop, Cornwell, and Inbar, "Catastrophic Geomorphic Processes and Bethsaida Archaeology, Israel," 165–69.

7. Rami Arav, "Bethsaida," in *Jesus and Archaeology*, ed. James H. Charlesworth (Grand Rapids, MI: William B. Eerdmans Pub. Co., 2006), 150.

8. Karl-Erich Wilken, *Biblisches Erleben Im Heiligen Land* (Lahr-Dinglingen: St.-Johannis-Druckerei C. Schweickhardt, 1953).

9. Arav, "Bethsaida," 150.

APPENDIX A
The Material Culture Database

In 2000, enabled by a grant from the Delmas Foundation, I began a project to create a digital record of the ceramic and small finds of the Bethsaida Excavation Project. This work was accomplished during 2000 and 2001 when the small finds that were collected on site during the 1990s and stored in the excavation office and facilities at the Beit Yigal Allon museum were scanned using a flatbed scanner and stored on compact discs. This method produced a low-cost high resolution record of the more interesting pottery, glass, coin, and other types of small finds and made it possible for researchers to have access to the material without being on site in Israel.

After the success of the small finds scanning project, work was also begun on creating a new database format that would record digitally photographs of all the diagnostic pieces that were processed during the daily pottery reading sessions held during the field season. Previously, the finds were recorded with verbal description, both by hand and by computer. The designated diagnostic pieces were then inscribed with basket and locus information, placed in tagged bags, and deposited in the Bethsaida pottery storage facility in the museum basement. If a researcher wanted to visually inspect the saved items, it was necessary, except for the few items that were drawn by the staff artist, to do so in person at the Israel excavation office. With the decreasing cost and increasing availability of digital cameras, I devised a methodology whereby each excavated basket[1] would be recorded digitally while being processed at the pottery reading and before being placed into storage.

This began by simply digitally photographing the saved ceramics and other material from each recorded basket. The finds were photographed together with the basket tag insuring that the finds were kept with their contextual link to the field notebook. A scale was provided by the spacing of the information lines on the tag; later a scale was printed directly on each basket tag. The idea was to insure easy access to material by researchers without necessitating laborious searches through the storage room to observe the diagnostic pieces. It was always intended to directly link the digital visual record to the excavation computer database.

Because Bethsaida already had a fairly sophisticated method of recording information on a computer database, this work on connecting the digital photographic record to the field notes and pottery reading information was begun with an idea of having backward compatibility with the ongoing database.[2] Unfortunately, because the original database was written in early DOS using a Hebrew variant of Microsoft DOS 4, this was not immediately possible. However, most of the same data elements were included in the newer database begun with this present research. The new database was designed to take advantage of a vastly improved Windows based graphics user interface. Chris Morton, a student at the University of Wisconsin at Eau Claire who was a member of the 2000 John and Carol Merrill Cave of Letters Expedition, and I began developing the database program that would become the standard method of recording information about the recovered material culture for the Bethsaida Excavation Project.[3] The idea was to incorporate the digital record along with the usual recording of the data elements such as basket number, locus, levels, finds, and descriptive elements of a day's activity in a particular locus. In this way, a researcher could access field notes, pottery reading, and the visual record of diagnostic finds, locus photos, and other data from a single computer database. I provided the outline of the program and its field testing while Chris did the tedious work of programming and coding the interface. On Chris's suggestion, we based the database framework on a Microsoft Access database and used Java for developing much of the interface.

Data input is accomplished via a data entry form that incorporates pull-down menus, data entry boxes, and the ability to easily modify and correct data entry mistakes—something that was very cumbersome in the old program. One can easily see all of the information included in each basket on one screen.[4] Figure A.1 shows a typical basket data entry screen.[5]

The Catalogue of Finds, shown as an entry field and pull-down menu under the category "Basket Finds" in figure A.1 and more fully under the heading "Select Search Criteria" on the search page at the bottom of figure A.1, was inherited from the previous database. While this insured compatibility with the earlier records, it also proved to be a limiting factor on data entry since one had to memorize the finds table to quickly input its information. However, modifications to the catalogue have enabled faster searching and recovery of the correct index code number and standard description of the more common types of pottery vessels. One can now type just a few letters of the index description and the search routine will quickly bring up the correct find type. Additionally a few coded abbreviations have been embedded to allow one to quickly reach a general pottery type. For example, typing "hcp" in the "search by index number" box when the alphabetic search option is selected will immediately point to "Hellenistic cooking pot." One can then select that generic description or quickly locate the more specific types by employing the pull-down menu.

Cross-referencing and report production was also a consideration when developing the database. Figure A.1 at the bottom shows the search screen where one is able to search the database by find type. One is able to search with various delimiters, such as by a date range, or by stratum. This enables the researcher to easily identify similar clusters of finds across the site or from previous years.

The annual report of the Bethsaida Excavation Project now includes a printout of the database information that includes the

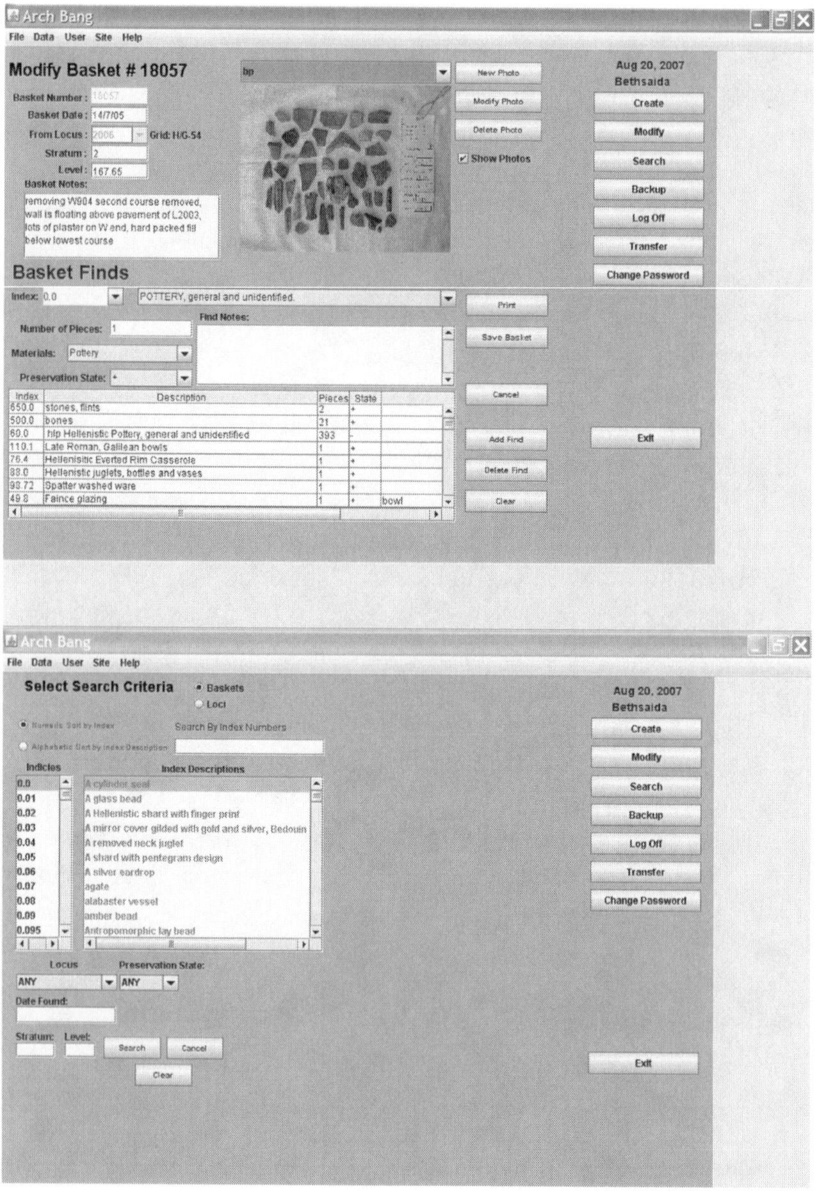

Figure A.1. Two Screenshots of the Bethsaida Database
Source: Author and Chris Morton, Software Architect (cosmo@cosmo.2y.net)

Bethsaida Basket # 18057 Report   20/8/07

Number	Date	Stratum	Level	Locus #
18057	14/7/05	2	167.65	2006

Basket Notes   **Grid**

removing W904 second course removed, wall is floating above pavement H/G-54
of L2003, lots of plaster on W end, hard packed fill below lowest course

Total Finds: 21

Index	Description	Qty	State	Materials	Find Notes
0.095	Plaster	1	-	Pottery	
49.8	Faince glazing	1	+	Pottery	bowl
60.0	hlp Hellenistic Pottery, general and unidentified	393	-	Pottery	
62.6	Hellenistic Decorated Ware	1	+	Pottery	
75.2	globular cooking pot, with lid device, L.72.1	3	+	Pottery	
75.2	globular cooking pot, with lid device, L.72.1	4	+	Pottery	
76.4	Hellenisitic Everted Rim Casserole	1	+	Pottery	
78.01	hlja Hellenistic Jar, general	1	+	Pottery	
78.01	hlja Hellenistic Jar, general	2	+	Pottery	
78.12	Hellenistic jar with double handle	1	+	Pottery	
88.0	Hellenistic juglets, bottles and vases	1	+	Pottery	
98.0	ETS, general and unidentified	1	+	Pottery	
98.72	Spatter washed ware	1	+	Pottery	
110.1	Late Roman, Galilean bowls	1	+	Pottery	
161.0	Medieval glazed pottery	2	+	Pottery	
161.0	Medieval glazed pottery	2	-	Pottery	
500.0	bones	21	+	Pottery	
650.0	stones, flints	2	+	Pottery	
830.0	Glass, Roman period	1	+	Pottery	bowl
830.0	Glass, Roman period	1	+	Pottery	
900.01	brick	1	-	Pottery	

Figure A.2.   Page One of a Database Basket Report
Source: Author and Chris Morton, Software Architect (cosmo@cosmo.2y.net)

photographic record. The reports are generated in a pdf format so that they can easily be transmitted digitally or printed. Figures A.2 and A.3 show a typical printout from one basket of recovered material. Figure A.2 is the printout of the recorded field notes and pottery reading data and figure A.3 includes the associated digital photographs of the specific material. Some baskets might also include a photograph of the material *in situ*.

Future modifications to the database will incorporate a digital map of the entire site so that one can produce maps showing where clusters of pottery types have been found or graphically display

Photos For Basket # 18057

2/11/05   Photo Name: bp

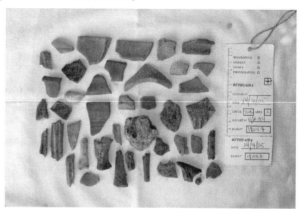

Source: C:\archbang\Images\baskets 2005_MG_5810.JPG
Description: bp

2/11/05   Photo Name: item

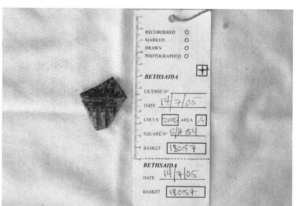

Source: C:\archbang\Images\baskets 2005_MG_5811.JPG
Description: bp

Figure A.3.   Page Two of a Database Basket Report
Source: Author and Chris Morton, Software Architect (cosmo@cosmo.2y.net)

where specific baskets of material have been excavated. This technique was first employed by the author with the Cave of Letters expedition. In the meantime, it is still necessary to manually locate loci and baskets on the site map. Also, online access to authorized users will be added in the next revision. The interface has been written to easily allow this adaptation.

While every modern expedition develops its own method for recording carefully controlled excavation data for maximum data retrieval using similar data elements that enable the recovery of the context for artifacts and architectural features, the database developed in conjunction with this research product is the first to incorporate the digital recording of all diagnostic finds. Thus it carries further the tradition of technical innovation in data recording begun by the expedition director, Rami Arav, in the mid 1990s.

NOTES

1. While the actual physical container used to temporarily store excavated artifacts is a bucket, "basket" is the terminology employed by the Bethsaida Excavations Project for the grouping of material recovered from a day's field work in a particular locus. Different excavations use different terminology to indicate how they group recovered material cultural units to ensure that their associated context is kept intact.

2. See Arav, "Bethsaida Excavations: Preliminary Report, 1994–1996," 4–10, for a detailed description of the previous database.

3. The database was also used for the Nazareth Bathhouse Excavation Project in 2005.

4. See figure A.1. The upper screenshot shows how the data entry screen would appear. One could click on the photo shown on that screen and enlarge it for better identification of the finds contained in the basket.

5. The Modify Screen and the Create Basket data entry screens are exactly the same. The only difference is that on the modify screen one is able to change previously entered data.

APPENDIX B

The Coin Database

A project similar to the one described in Appendix 1, which detailed the Material Finds Database, was the development of the Coin Database. The initial concept for this database was developed by the author, but his initial efforts were modified by Chris Hertzler, a volunteer who worked on this project during the off season 2001–2002. He created the basic design of the database interface and began the tedious process of entering the data from Dr. Kindler's coin reports.

I completed the data entry in 2005 and added scans of all of the available coins to the database, so that we now have a complete record of each coin that has been excavated by the Bethsaida Excavations Project. The database is updated yearly as the coins are returned from cleaning and analysis.

Figure B.1 shows a typical coin report in the database. There are three screens available for each coin. The first (bottom) includes general information about the coin from the field notes, including the contextual information of where it was found on the site. A second screen (middle) contains the detailed information from the numismatist. A third screen (top) contains the scan of the coin's obverse and reverse. While the photographs are not a replacement for actual examination for identification purposes by other researchers,

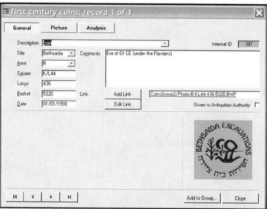

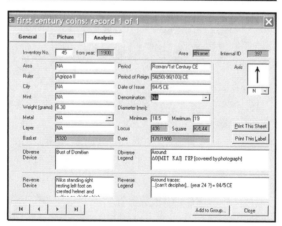

Figure B.1.   Screenshots of the Coin Database
Source: Author and Chris Hetzler

they serve to allow one a better appreciation for the condition and depiction of a coin than would be available from the numismatic descriptions alone.

The database allows the researcher to group the coins by date, type, or almost any other criterion that is desired. Thus tagged, a coin can readily be recalled with others in its group. This database provides a wonderful resource that is readily accessible to the researcher. Presently, the coin database with all of its associated digital scans readily fits on a single CD.

BIBLIOGRAPHY

Adan-Bayewitz, David. *Common Pottery in Roman Galilee: A Study of Local Trade.* Bar-Ilan Studies in Near Eastern Languages and Culture. Ramat-Gan, Israel: Bar-Ilan University Press, 1993.

———. "Kafr Hananya—1987." In *Excavations and Surveys in Israel 7–8.* Jerusalem: Israel Dept. of Antiquities and Museums, 1988/89.

Alt, Albrecht. "Galiläische Probleme." In *Kleine Schriften Zur Geschichte Des Volkes Israel,* 2:363–465. München: C. H. Beck, 1953.

Andersen, F. G., and James F. Strange. "Bericht Über Drei Sondagen Im Umm Qais, Jordanien, Im Herbst 1983." *Zeitschrift Des Deutschen Palästina-Vereins* 103 (1987): 90–92, plate 11.6.

Applebaum, Shimon. "Judaea as a Roman Province; the Countryside as a Political and Economic Factor." *Aufstieg und Niedergang der Römischen Welt (ANRW)* II, no. 8 (1977): 355–96.

Arav, Rami. "Bethsaida Excavations: Preliminary Report, 1987–1993." Pp. 3–113 in *The Bethsaida Excavations Project Reports & Contextual Studies.* Edited by Rami Arav. Kirksville, MO: Thomas Jefferson University Press, 1995.

———. "Bethsaida Excavations: Preliminary Report, 1994–1996." Pp. 3–63 in *The Bethsaida Excavations Project Reports & Contextual Studies.* Edited by Rami Arav. Kirksville, MO: Thomas Jefferson University Press, 1999.

———. "Bethsaida." Pp. 145–66 in *Jesus and Archaeology.* Edited by James H. Charlesworth. Grand Rapids, MI: William B. Eerdmans, 2006.

———. Personal email, 2007.

———. "Towards a Comprehensive History of Geshur." In *The Bethsaida Excavations Project Reports & Contextual Studies, Vol.* 3. Edited by Rami Arav. Kirksville, MO: Thomas Jefferson University Press, 2004.

Ariel, Donald T. *Excavations at the City of David 1978–1985 Directed by Yigal Shiloh, Vol. II: Imported Stamped Amphora Handles, Coins, Worked Bone and Ivory, and Glass.* Qedem 30. Jerusalem: Institute of Archaeology, Hebrew University of Jerusalem, 1990.

———. "Stamped Amphora Handles from Bethsaida." In *The Bethsaida Excavations Project Reports & Contextual Studies, Vol.* 4. Edited by Rami Arav. Kirksville, MO: Thomas Jefferson University Press, 2009.

Aviam, Mordechai. "Distribution Maps of Archaeological Data in the Galilee as an Attempt to Create Ethnic and Religion Zones." Conference presentation. Ancient Galilee in Interaction: Religion, Ethnicity, and Identity. Yale University, 2004.

———. "First Century Jewish Galilee." In *Religion and Society in Roman Palestine: Old Questions, New Approaches.* Edited by Douglas R. Edwards. New York: Routledge, 2004.

———. *Jews, Pagans, and Christians in the Galilee: 25 Years of Archaeological Excavations and Surveys: Hellenistic to Byzantine Periods.* Rochester, NY: University of Rochester Press, 2004.

Avigad, Nahman. *Discovering Jerusalem.* Nashville, TN: T. Nelson, 1983.

Avi-Yonah, Michael. "Syrian Gods at Ptolemais-Akko." *Israel Exploration Journal*, no. 9 (1959): 1–12.

Bagatti, Bellarmino. "Scavo Presso la Chiesa di San Giuseppe a Nazaret." *Liber Annuus* (1971).

Batey, Richard A. "Is Not This the Carpenter?" *New Testament Studies* 30, no. 2 (1984): 249–58.

———. *Jesus and the Forgotten City: New Light on Sepphoris and the Urban World of Jesus.* Grand Rapids, MI: Baker Book House, 1991.

Bauer, Walter. "Jesus der Galiläer." Pp. 91–108 in *Aufsätze und Kleine Schriften.* Edited by Georg Strecker. Tübingen: Mohr Siebeck, 1967.

Berlin, Andrea M. "From Monarchy to Markets: The Phoenicians in Hellenistic Palestine." *Bulletin of the American Schools of Oriental Research* 306 (May 1997): 75–88.

———. *Gamla I: The Pottery of the Second Temple Period, the Shmarya Gutmann Excavations, 1976–1989.* IAA Reports. Jerusalem: Israel Antiquities Authority, 2006.

———. "The Hellenistic Period." Pp. 418–33 in *Near Eastern Archaeology: A Reader.* Edited by Suzanne Richard. Winona Lake, IN: Eisenbrauns, 2003.

———. *Jewish Life before the Revolt: The Archaeological Evidence.* Papers of the SBL Josephus Seminar, 1999–2004, 2004. http://pace.cns.yorku.ca:8080/media/pdf/sbl/Berlin%20Archaeology.pdf (accessed August 23, 2007).

———. "The Plain Wares." Pp. 1–211 in *The Hellenistic and Roman Pottery.* Edited by Sharon C. Herbert. Ann Arbor, MI: Kelsey Museum of the University of Michigan, 1997.

Binder, Donald D. *Into the Temple Courts the Place of the Synagogues in the Second Temple Period.* Atlanta, GA: Society of Biblical Literature, 1999.

Binford, Lewis Roberts, John F. Cherry, and Robin Torrence. *In Pursuit of the Past: Decoding the Archaeological Record.* Edited by John F. Cherry. New York and London: Thames and Hudson, 1983.

Boobyer, G. H. *Galilee and Galileans in St. Mark's Gospel*, 1953.

Börker, Christoph. "Der Pergamon-Komplex." In *Die Hellenistischen Amphorenstempel Aus Pergamon*, 3–69. Berlin, 1998.

Brandl, Baruch. "Two First-Millennium Cylinder Seals from Bethsaida (Et-Tell)." In *Bethsaida: A City by the North Shore of the Sea of Galilee*, 225–44. Kirksville, MO: Truman State University Press, 1999.

Briant, Pierre. *From Cyrus to Alexander: A History of the Persian Empire.* Winona Lake, IN: Eisenbrauns, 2002.

Broshi, Magen. "The Role of the Temple in the Herodian Economy." *The Journal of Jewish Studies* 38, no. 1 (Spring 1987).

Brown, Francis, et al. *The Brown-Driver-Briggs Hebrew and English Lexicon with an Appendix Containing the Biblical Aramaic: Coded with the Numbering System from Strong's Exhaustive Concordance of the Bible.* Peabody, MA: Hendrickson Publishers, 1996.

Cahill, Jane M. "Chalk Assemblages of the Persian/Hellenistic and Early Roman Periods." In *Qedem 33*, 190–274. Jerusalem: Institute of Archaeology, Hebrew University of Jerusalem, 1992.

Carter, Charles E. "Syria-Palestine in the Persian Period." In *Near Eastern Archaeology: A Reader.* Edited by Suzanne Richard. Winona Lake, IN: Eisenbrauns, 2003.

Chancey, Mark A. *The Myth of a Gentile Galilee: The Population of Galilee and New Testament Studies.* New York: Cambridge University Press, 2002.

Chancey, Mark A., and Adam L. Porter. "The Archaeology of Roman Palestine." In *Near Eastern Archaeology.*, 164–203. Atlanta, GA: Published by Scholars Press for the American Schools of Oriental Research, 2001.

Chen, Doron. "The Design of the Ancient Synagogues in Judea: Masada and Herodium." In *Bulletin of the American Schools of Oriental Research*, 37–40. Missoula, MT: Scholars Press, 1980.

Choi, Agnes. "The Traveling Peasant and Urban-Rural Relations in Roman Galilee." Canadian Society of Biblical Studies Seminar. University of Western Ontario, London, Ontario, 2005. http://www.philipharland .com/travel/TravelChoiGalilee.pdf (accessed August 23, 2007).

Cohen, Shaye J. D. *From the Maccabees to the Mishnah*. Library of Early Christianity. Philadelphia: Westminster Press, 1987.

Conovici, N., and M. Irimia. "Timbres Amphoriques et Autres Inscriptions Céramiques Découverts à Satu Nou." *Dacia: Revue d'Archéologie et d'Histoire Ancienne* 35 (1991): 139–75.

Crossan, John Dominic, and Jonathan L. Reed. *Excavating Jesus Beneath the Stones, Behind the Texts*. San Francisco: HarperSanFrancisco, 2001.

Díez Fernández, Florentino. *Cerámica Común Romana de la Galilea Aproximaciones y Diferencias con la Cerámica del Resto de Palestina y Regiones Circundantes*. Madrid: Ed. Biblia y Fé Escuela Bíblica, 1983.

Edwards, Douglas R. "First Century Urban/Rural Relations in Lower Galilee: Exploring Archaeological and Literary Evidence." *Society of Biblical Literature Seminar Papers* 27 (1988): 169–82.

———. "The Socio-Economic and Cultural Ethos of the Lower Galilee in the First Century: Implications for the Nascent Jesus Movement." Pp. 53–73 in *The Galilee in Late Antiquity*. Edited by Lee I. Levine. New York and Cambridge, MA: Jewish Theological Seminary of America Distributed by Harvard University Press, 1992.

Elayi, Josette, and Jean Sapin. *Beyond the River: New Perspectives on Transeuphratene*. Journal for the Study of the Old Testament. Sheffield, England: Sheffield Academic Press, 1998.

Elliott-Binns, Leonard. *Galilean Christianity*. Chicago: A. R. Allenson, 1956.

Finegan, Jack. *Light from the Ancient Past: The Archeological Background of Judaism and Christianity*. Princeton, NJ: Princeton University Press, 1959.

Finkelstein, Israel. *The Archaeology of the Israelite Settlement*. Jerusalem: Israel Exploration Society, 1988.

Finkelstein, Israel, and Neil Asher Silberman. *David and Solomon in Search of the Bible's Sacred Kings and the Roots of the Western Tradition*. New York: Free Press, 2006.

Finkielsztejn, Gérald. "Amphoras and Stamped Handles from 'Akko'." *Atiqot: Journal of the Israel Department of Antiquities* 39 (2000): 135–53.

———. *Chronologie Détaillée et Révisée Des Éponymes Amphoriques Rhodiens, de 270 à 108 av. J.-C. Environ Premier Bilan*. Oxford, England: Archaeopress, 2001.

————. "Politique et Commerce à Rhodes au IIe s. a.C.: Le Témoignage Des Exportations d'Amphores." In *Les Cités d'Asie Mineure Occidentale au IIe Siècle a.C*, 181–91. Bordeaux: Ausonius-Publications, 2001.

Fisher, Toni. "This Close to Publishing My Dissertation: Bones Update." Batchelder Biblical Archaeological Conference. Omaha, NE, 2002.

————. "The Zooarchaeological Implications of et-Tel/Bethsaida from the Iron Age to Early Roman Periods." Unpublished dissertation. Knoxville, TN: University of Tennessee, 2005.

Flannery, Kent V., and Joyce Marcus. "Cognitive Archaeology." Pp. 350–63 in *Contemporary Archaeology in Theory: A Reader*. Edited by Robert W. Preucel. Social Archaeology. Cambridge, MA: Blackwell, 1996.

Foester, Gideon. "The Synagogues at Masada and Herodium." Pp. 24–29 in *Ancient Synagogues Revealed*. Edited by Lee I. Levine. Jerusalem: Israel Exploration Society, 1982.

Fortner, Sandra Ann. "Die Keramik und Kleinfunde von Bethsaida Am See Genezareth, Israel." Unpublished dissertation. University of Munich, 2005.

Frankel, Rafi. *Settlement Dynamics and Regional Diversity in Ancient Upper Galilee: Archaeological Survey of Upper Galilee*. IAA Reports. Jerusalem: Israel Antiquities Authority, 2001.

Freund, Richard A. "The Incense Shovel of Bethsaida and Synagogue Iconography in Late Antiquity." Pp. 413–59 in *The Bethsaida Excavations Project Reports & Contextual Studies*. Edited by Rami Arav. Kirksville, MO: Thomas Jefferson University Press, 1999.

————. "The Tannery of Bethsaida?" Pp. 233–52 in *The Bethsaida Excavations Project Reports & Contextual Studies, Vol. 3*. Edited by Rami Arav. Kirksville, MO: Truman State University Press, 2004.

Freyne, Sean. "Galilean Studies: Old Issues and New Questions." Pp. 13–29 in *Religion, Ethnicity, and Identity in Ancient Galilee*. Edited by Jürgen Zangenberg, Harold W. Attridge, and Dale B. Martin. Wissenschaftliche Untersuchungen Zum Neuen Testament. Tübingen: Mohr Siebeck, 2007.

————. "Galileans." Pp. 876–78 in *Anchor Bible Dictionary Vol. 2*. New York: Doubleday, 1992.

————. *Galilee, from Alexander the Great to Hadrian, 323 B.C.E. to 135 C.E. a Study of Second Temple Judaism*. Wilmington, DE, and Notre Dame, IN: M. Glazier University of Notre Dame Press, 1980.

————. "Galilee-Jerusalem Relations According to Josephus' Life." *New Testament Studies* 33 (1987): 600–09.

————. "Hellenistic/Roman Galilee." In *Anchor Bible Dictionary Volume 2*, 895–99. New York: Doubleday, 1992.

———. "Jesus and the Urban Culture of Galilee." Pp. 597–622 in *Text and Contexts Biblical Texts in Their Textual and Situational Contexts: Essays in Honor of Lars Hartman*. Edited by Tord Fornberg. Oslo and Boston: Scandinavian University Press, 1995.

———. "Urban-Rural Relations in First-Century Galilee." Pp. 75–91 in *The Galilee in Late Antiquity*. Edited by Lee I. Levine. New York and Cambridge, MA: Jewish Theological Seminary of America distributed by Harvard University Press, 1992.

Fried, Lisbeth S. *The Priest and the Great King Temple-Palace Relations in the Persian Empire*. Winona Lake, IN: Eisenbrauns, 2004.

Funk, Robert Walter. *Honest to Jesus: Jesus for a New Millennium*. San Francisco, CA: HarperSanFrancisco, 1996.

Gal, Zvi. *Lower Galilee During the Iron Age*. Winona Lake, IN: Eisenbrauns, 1992.

Goldstein, Jonathan A. *I Maccabees: A New Translation, with Introduction and Commentary*. Anchor Bible. Garden City, NY: Doubleday, 1976.

Golinkin, David. "Prayers for the Government." *Insight Israel* 6, no. 9 (May 2006).

Goodman, Martin. "The First Jewish Revolt: Social Conflict and the Problem of Debt." *The Journal of Jewish Studies* 33 (1982): 417–27.

Groh, Dennis E. "The Clash Between Literary and Archaeological Models." In *Archaeology and the Galilee Texts and Contexts in the Graeco-Roman and Byzantine Periods*, 29–37. Atlanta, GA: Scholars Press, 1997.

Grootkerk, Salomon E. *Ancient Sites in Galilee: A Toponymic Gazetteer*. Culture and History of the Ancient Near East. Leiden and Boston: Brill, 2000.

Gutman, Shemaryah. *Gamla Ha-Hafirot Bi-Shemoneh Ha- Onot Ha-Rishonah*. Tel-Aviv: Hotsa at ha-Kibuts ha-me uhad, 1981.

Gutmann, Shmaryahu. "Gamala." Pp. 459–63 in *The New Encyclopedia of Archaeological Excavations in the Holy Land*. Edited by Ephraim Stern. Jerusalem: Israel Exploration Society & Carta; New York: Simon & Schuster, 1993.

Havernick, Th. E. "Nadelköpfe Vom Typ Kempten." *Germania* 50 (1972): 136–48.

Hengel, Martin. *Judaism and Hellenism Studies in Their Encounter in Palestine During the Early Hellenistic Period*. London: SCM Press, 1974.

Herbert, Sharon C., and Donald T. Ariel. *Tel Anafa I: Final Report on Ten Years of Excavation at a Hellenistic and Roman Settlement in Northern Israel*. Journal of Roman Archaeology. Ann Arbor, MI: Kelsey Museum of the University of Michigan, 1994.

Herbert, Sharon C., Leslie A. Cornell, Andrea M. Berlin, and Kathleen W. Slane. *The Hellenistic and Roman Pottery*. Edited by Sharon C. Herbert. Tel Anafa. Ann Arbor, MI: Kelsey Museum of the University of Michigan, 1997.

Hoglund, Kenneth G. *Achaemenid Imperial Administration in Syria-Palestine and the Missions of Ezra and Nehemiah*. Atlanta, GA: Scholars Press, 1992.

Horsley, Richard A. *Galilee History, Politics, People*. Valley Forge, PA: Trinity Press International, 1995.

Isings, C. *Roman Glass from Dated Finds*. Archaeologica Traiectina. Groningen: J. B. Wolters, 1957.

Jöhrens, Gerhard. *Amphorenstempel Im Nationalmuseum von Athen zu Den von H.G. Lolling Aufgenommenen "Unedierten Henkelinschriften."* Mainz: In Kommission bei P. von Zabern, 1999.

Josephus, Flavius. *The Works of Flavius Josephus, Volume II*. Translated by William Whiston. Nashville, TN: Baker Book House, 1974.

Kee, Howard Clark. *Community of the New Age: Studies in Mark's Gospel*. Philadelphia: Westminster Press, 1977.

Koester, Helmut. *Introduction to the New Testament*. New York: Walter de Gruyter, 1995.

Leibner, Uzi. "History of Settlement in the Eastern Galilee During the Hellenistic, Roman and Byzantine Periods in Light of an Archaeological Survey." PhD dissertation. Ramet-Gan, Israel: Bar-Ilan University, 2004.

———. "Settlement and Demography in Late Roman and Byzantine Eastern Galilee." Pp. 105–30 in *Settlements and Demography in the Near East in Late Antiquity: Proceedings of the Colloquium, Matera, 27–29 October 2005*. Edited by Ariel Lewin. Biblioteca di Mediterraneo Antico. Pisa: Istituti editoriali e poligrafici internazionali, 2006.

Loffreda, Stanislao. *Cafarnao 2: La Ceramica*. Jerusalem: Francescani, 1974.

———. *La Sinagoga di Cafarnao, Dopo Gli Scavi del 1969*. Jerusalem: Francescani, 1970.

Loftus, Francis. "The Anti-Roman Revolts of the Jews and the Galileans." *The Jewish Quarterly Review* 68, no. 2 (October 1977): 78–98.

Mack, Burton L. *The Lost Gospel: The Book of Q & Christian Origins*. San Francisco: HarperSanFrancisco, 1993.

Magen, Yitzhak. *The Stone Vessel Industry in the Second Temple Period*. Jerusalem: Israel Exploration Society, 2002.

Magness, Jodi. "Did Galilee Decline in the Fifth Century?" Ancient Galilee in Interaction: Religion, Ethnicity, and Identity. Yale University, 2004.

Malherbe, Abraham J. "Life in the Greco-Roman World." Pp. 4–36 in *The World of the New Testament*. Austin, TX: R.B. Sweet Co., Inc., 1967.

Manns, Frédéric. "A Survey of Recent Studies on Early Christianity." Pp. 17–25 in *Early Christianity in Context Monuments and Documents*. Edited by Frédéric Manns. Jerusalem: Franciscan Printing Press, 1993.

Mazar, Amihai. *Archaeology of the Land of the Bible: 10,000–586 B.C.E.* Anchor Bible Reference Library. New York: Doubleday, 1990.

McNamer, Elizabeth. "Medieval Pilgrim Accounts of Bethsaida and the Bethsaida Controversy." Pp. 397–412 in *The Bethsaida Excavations Project Reports & Contextual Studies*. Edited by Rami Arav. Kirksville, MO: Thomas Jefferson University Press, 1999.

Meier, John P. *A Marginal Jew: Rethinking the Historical Jesus*. The Anchor Bible Reference Library. New York: Doubleday, 1991.

Meshorer, Ya akov. *A Treasury of Jewish Coins: From the Persian Period to Bar Kokhba*. Nyack: Amphora, 2001.

Meyers, Eric M. "Aspects of Roman Sepphoris in the Light of Recent Archaeology." Pp. 29–36 in *Aspects of Roman Sepphoris in the Light of Recent Archaeology*. Edited by Frédéric Manns. Jerusalem: Franciscan Printing Press, 1993.

———. "Galilean Regionalism as a Factor in Historical Reconstruction." *Bulletin of the American Schools of Oriental Research* 221 (1976): 93–102.

———. "Jesus and His Galilean Context." In *Archaeology and the Galilee: Texts and Contexts in the Graeco-Roman and Byzantine Periods*. Atlanta, GA: Scholars Press, 1997.

———. "Roman Sepphoris in Light of New Archaeological Evidence and Recent Research." Pp. 321–38 in *The Galilee in Late Antiquity*. Edited by Lee I. Levine. New York and Cambridge, MA: Jewish Theological Seminary of America distributed by Harvard University Press, 1992.

Meyers, Eric M., James F. Strange, and Carol L. Meyers. *Excavations at Ancient Meiron, Upper Galilee, Israel, 1971–72; 1974–74; 1977*. Cambridge, MA: American Schools of Oriental Research, 1981.

Miller, Stuart S. "Some Observations on Stone Vessel Finds and Ritual Purity in Light of Talmudic Sources." In *Zeichen Aus Text und Stein*. Edited by Stefan Alkier and Jürgen Zangenberg. Tübingen: Francke Verlag, 2003.

Moxnes, Halvor. "The Construction of Galilee as a Place for the Historical Jesus—Part II." *Biblical Theology Bulletin*, Summer 2001.

Negev, Avraham. *The Late Hellenistic and Early Roman Pottery of Nabatean Oboda.* Qedem 22. Jerusalem: Institute of Archaeology, Hebrew University of Jerusalem, 1986.

Netzer, Ehud. *Greater Herodium.* Qedem 13. Jerusalem: Institute of Archaeology, Hebrew University of Jerusalem, 1981.

Nowogórski, Przemyslaw. "Protosynagoga W Betsaidzie: Hipotetyczna Interpretacja Budynku Na Area A Na Et-Tell (Betsaida)." Pp. 41–47 in *Studia Judaica Biuletyn Polskiego Towarzystwa Studiów Zydowskich.* Kraków: Ksiegarnia Akademicka, 2004.

Oakman, Douglas E. "The Archaeology of First-Century Galilee and the Social Interpretation of the Historical Jesus." In *Society of Biblical Literature Seminar Papers,* 220–51. Missoula, MT: Scholars Press, 1994.

Overman, Andrew J. "Jesus of Galilee and the Historical Present." In *Archaeology and the Galilee: Texts and Contexts in the Graeco-Roman and Byzantine Periods,* 67–73. Atlanta, GA: Scholars Press, 1997.

Perkins, Pheme. *Reading the New Testament: An Introduction.* New York: Paulist Press, 1988.

Peters, F. E. *The Harvest of Hellenism a History of the Near East from Alexander the Great to the Triumph of Christianity.* New York: Simon and Schuster, 1971.

Preucel, Robert W., and Ian Hodder. *Contemporary Archaeology in Theory: A Reader.* Edited by Robert W. Preucel. Social Archaeology. Cambridge, MA: Blackwell, 1996.

Radulescu, A., M. Barbulescu, and L. Buzoianu. "Importuri Amforice la Albesti (Jud. Constanta): Rhodes." *Pontica* 20 (1987): 79–106.

Redding, Richard W. "The Vertebrate Fauna." In *Tel Anafa I,* Journal of Roman Archaeology. Ann Arbor, MI: Kelsey Museum of the University of Michigan, 1994.

Redfield, R., R. Linton, and M. J. Herskovits. "Memorandum for the Study of Acculturation." In *American Anthropologist.* Washington, DC: American Anthropological Association, 1936.

Redfield, Robert, and Milton Singer. "The Cultural Role of Cities." In *Economic Development and Cultural Change,* 53–73. Chicago: University of Chicago Press, 1954.

Reed, Jonathan L. *Archaeology and the Galilean Jesus: A Re-Examination of the Evidence.* Harrisburg, PA: Trinity Press International, 2000.

———. "Galileans, 'Israelite Village Communities,' and the Sayings Gospel Q." Pp. 87–108 in *Galilee Through the Centuries: Confluence of Cultures.*

Edited by Eric M. Meyers. Duke Judaic Studies Series. Winona Lake, IN: Eisenbrauns, 1999.

Reeder, Philip, Harry Jol, Richard Freund, and Carl Savage. "Geoarchaeology of the Qumran Archaeological Site, Israel." *Focus on Geography* 48, no. 1 (Summer 2004): 12–19.

Reicke, Bo Ivar. *The New Testament Era: The World of the Bible from 500 B.C. to A.D. 100.* Philadelphia: Fortress Press, 1968.

Robinson, James McConkey, and Helmut Koester. *Trajectories through Early Christianity.* Philadelphia: Fortress Press, 1971.

Rosenthal, Renate, and Renee Sivan. *Ancient Lamps in the Schloessinger Collection.* Qedem 8. Jerusalem: Institute of Archaeology, Hebrew University of Jerusalem, 1978.

Rottloff, Andrea. "Hellenistic, Roman and Islamic Glass from Bethsaida (*Iulias*, Israel)." *Annuals of the 14th Congress of the International Association for the History of Glass* (2000). Lochem, Netherlands: AIHV.

Safrai, Zeev. "The Roman Army in the Galilee." Pp. 103–14 in *The Galilee in Late Antiquity.* Edited by Lee I. Levine. New York and Cambridge, MA: Jewish Theological Seminary of America Distributed by Harvard University Press, 1992.

Saldarini, Anthony J. *Matthew's Christian-Jewish Community.* Chicago Studies in the History of Judaism. Chicago: University of Chicago Press, 1994.

Sanders, E. P. "Jesus' Galilee." Pp. 3–42 in *Fair Play Diversity and Conflicts in Early Christianity: Essays in Honour of Heikki Räisänen.* Supplements to Novum Testamentum. Leiden and Boston: Brill, 2002.

Savage, Carl. "Revisiting the Temple at Bethsaida." Society for Biblical Literature. Philadelphia, 2006.

Sawicki, Marianne. *Crossing Galilee: Architectures of Contact in the Occupied Land of Jesus.* Harrisburg, PA: Trinity Press International, 2000.

———. "Spatial Management of Gender and Labor." Pp. 7–28 in *Archaeology and the Galilee: Texts and Contexts in the Graeco-Roman and Byzantine Periods.* Atlanta, GA: Scholars Press, 1997.

Schoville, Keith N. *Biblical Archaeology in Focus.* Grand Rapids: Baker Book House, 1978.

Schuchhardt, Carl. "Amphorenstempel." Pp. 423–98 in *Die Inschriften von Pergamon 2, Römische Zeit-Inschriften auf Thon Altertümer von Pergamon VIII, 2.* Berlin: W. Spemann, 1895.

Schürer, Emil, Géza Vermès, and Fergus Millar. *The History of the Jewish People in the Age of Jesus Christ (175 B.C.–A.D. 135).* Edited by Géza Vermès. Edinburgh: Clark, 1973.

Segal, Arthur. *Hippos-Sussita Fifth Season of Excavations: September-October 2004*. Haifa: Zinman Institute of Archaeology, University of Haifa, 2004.

———. "The Spade Hits Sussita." *The Biblical Archaeology Review* 32 (May/June 2006): 40–60.

Shachar, Ilan. "The Later Coinage of Alexander Jannaeus and Its Historical Implications." Unpublished MA thesis. Tel Aviv University, 2002.

Shroder, Jack F., Michael Bishop, Kevin J. Cornwell, and Moshe Inbar. "Catastrophic Geomorphic Processes and Bethsaida Archaeology, Israel." Pp. 115–73 in *The Bethsaida Excavations Project Reports & Contextual Studies*. Edited by Rami Arav. Kirksville, MO: Thomas Jefferson University Press, 1999.

Shroder, Jack F., and Moshe Inbar. "Geologic and Geographic Background to the Bethsaida Excavations." Pp. 65–98 in *The Bethsaida Excavations Project Reports & Contextual Studies*. Edited by Rami Arav. Kirksville, MO: Thomas Jefferson University Press, 1995.

Simons, Jan Jozef. *Handbook for the Study of Egyptian Topographical Lists Relating to Western Asia*. Leiden: E. J. Brill, 1937.

Smith, Jonathan Z. *To Take Place: Toward Theory in Ritual*. Chicago Studies in the History of Judaism. Chicago: University of Chicago Press, 1987.

Smith, Robert Houston, and Leslie Preston Day. *Pella of the Decapolis*. Wooster, OH: College of Wooster, 1973.

Stark, Miriam T. "Technical Choices and Social Boundaries in Material Culture Patterning: An Introduction." Pp. 1–11 in *The Archaeology of Social Boundaries*. Edited by Miriam T. Stark. Smithsonian Series in Archaeological Inquiry. Washington, DC: Smithsonian Institution Press, 1998.

Stern, Edna J. "'Araba." *Excavations and Surveys in Israel* 18, no. 106 (1998): 15, (22–24 Heb.).

Stern, Ephraim. *Archaeology of the Land of the Bible: The Assyrian, Babylonian, and Persian Periods, 732–332 BCE*. Anchor Bible Reference Library. New York: Doubleday, 2001.

———. "A Favissa of a Phoenician Sanctuary from Tel Dor." Pp. 35–54 in *The Journal of Jewish Studies*. Cambridge, England, 1982.

Strange, James F. Batchelder Biblical Archaeology Conference, conversation with the author. Batchelder Biblical Archaeology Conference. University of Nebraska at Omaha, 2004, 22–24 October.

———. *Sepphoris and Galilee in Josephus' Vita*. Papers of the SBL Josephus Seminar, 1999–2004, 2001. http://pace.cns.yorku.ca:8080/media/pdf/sbl/strange2001.pdf (accessed August 23, 2007).

Strickert, Frederick M. *Bethsaida: Home of the Apostles*. Collegeville, MN: Liturgical Press, 1998.

Syon, Danny, and Zvi Yavor. "Gamla Old and New." *Qadmoniot* 34, no. 1 (2001).

Tappy, Ron E., et al. "An Abecedary of the Mid-Tenth Century B.C.E." *Bulletin of the American Schools of Oriental Research* 344 (November 2006): 5–46.

Tsaferis, Vasillios. "The Ancient Cemetery of Akko-Ptolemais." In *The Western Galilee Antiquities*, 266 ff. Tel Aviv, Israel: Misrad ha-bitahon ha-Moatsah ha-ezorit Mateh Asher, ha-Hug ha-ezori li-yedi at ha-Arets, 1986.

Urman, Dan. "The Public Structures and Jewish Communities in the Golan Heights." Pp. 373–651 in *Ancient Synagogues Historical Analysis and Archaeological Data*. Edited by Dan Urman and Paul V. M. Flesher. Studia Post-Biblica. Leiden New York: E. J. Brill, 1995.

Vaage, Leif E. *Galilean Upstarts: Jesus' First Followers According to Q*. Valley Forge, PA: Trinity Press International, 1994.

Wall, Robert W. "The Acts of The Apostles." Pp. 1–368 in *The New Interpreter's Bible, Volume X*. Nashville: Abingdon, 2002.

Weinberg, G. D. "Hellenistic Glass from Tel Anafa in Upper Galilee." *Journal of Glass Studies* 12 (1970): 17–27.

Wesley, John. *Explanatory Notes Upon the New Testament*. Grand Rapids, MI: Baker Book House, 1745, reprinted 1981.

Wilken, Karl-Erich. *Biblisches Erleben Im Heiligen Land*. Lahr-Dinglingen: St.-Johannis-Druckerei C. Schweickhardt, 1953.

Wilson, H. W. "Galilee." *A Guide to the Ancient World* (1986). www.credoreference.com/entry/5073300 (accessed August 13, 2007).

Wolfinger, Kirk. *Ancient Refuge in the Holy Land*. Gary Hochman. NOVA. Nebraska Educational Telecommunications for WGBH/Boston, 2004.

Younker, Randall W. "The Iron Age in the Southern Levant." In *Near Eastern Archaeology: A Reader*. Edited by Suzanne Richard. Winona Lake, IN: Eisenbrauns, 2003.

INDEX

ABOUT THE AUTHOR

Carl E. Savage is currently director of the Drew DMIN program. He began teaching at Drew's Theological School in the fall of 1999, where he received his PhD with distinction. His educational background is in biblical interpretation as well as sociology of religion, the origins of Christianity, and archaeology. He is a registered professional archaeologist and serves as the assistant director of excavations for the Bethsaida Excavations Project. His excavation experience also includes work at the Cave of Letters, Qumran, Nazereth, and Yavne. He has written numerous articles in the field of archaeology including, "Supporting Evidence for a First-Century Bethsaida," in *Religion, Ethnicity and Identity in Ancient Galilee: A Region in Transition*, edited by Jürgen Zangenberg, Harold W. Attridge, and Dale B. Martin (Tübingen: Mohr Siebeck, 2007) and "The Leshem Inscription" in *Bethsaida: A City by the North Shore of the Sea of Galilee*, volume IV, edited by Rami Arav and Richard A. Freund (Kirksville, MO: Thomas Jefferson University Press, 2010). Dr. Savage has appeared in the Nova special, *Ancient Refuge in the Holy Land* (2004) and in the Biblical Archaeological Society's "Refuge in the Cave of Letters: A Report from the John P. and Carol Merrill Expedition to the Cave of the Letters," part of *Lecture Series Volume I: Just Dug Up: The Latest Finds from Biblical Israel and the Deep*.